My Abstract Life

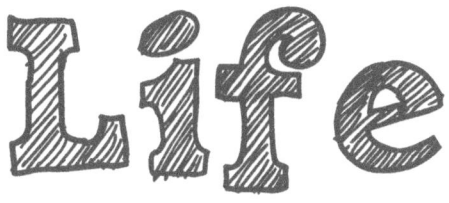

Poetry and Paintings

Paul Klinger

Including poetry by Cheryl Perlow

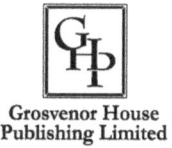

Grosvenor House
Publishing Limited

All rights reserved
Copyright © Paul Klinger, 2018

The right of Paul Klinger to be identified as the author of this
work has been asserted in accordance with Section 78
of the Copyright, Designs and Patents Act 1988

The book cover picture is copyright to Paul Klinger

This book is published by
Grosvenor House Publishing Ltd
Link House
140 The Broadway, Tolworth, Surrey, KT6 7HT.
www.grosvenorhousepublishing.co.uk

This book is sold subject to the conditions that it shall not, by way of
trade or otherwise, be lent, resold, hired out or otherwise circulated
without the author's or publisher's prior consent in any form of binding or
cover other than that in which it is published and
without a similar condition including this condition being imposed
on the subsequent purchaser.

This book is a work of fiction. Any resemblance to
people or events, past or present, is purely coincidental.

A CIP record for this book
is available from the British Library

ISBN 978-1-78623-137-6

Dedication:

This book is dedicated to the memory of my cousin Cheryl Perlow.

Contents

INTRODUCTION ix
CHAPTER 1 1
   THE MAN AND WOMAN IN THE PICTURE 2
   IN THE SHADOW OF THE SHARD 3
   PEOPLE 4
   THE CONCENTRIC CIRCLES 5
   THE COUNTRY SQUIRE 7
CHAPTER 2 9
   MY DAY – A SAGA 9
      Driving to work 11
      The working day 12
      Lunch time 14
      The afternoon 15
      The Evening 16
   THE MISSIONARY COLLEGE 18
   TRAVELLING ON THE TUBE 20
   CELESTE 21
   BREAKFAST IN THE HOTEL 23
CHAPTER 3 25
   THE HORSE AND THE MAGPIE 25
   FROM MY HOTEL WINDOW 29

THE DAY THE PIER BURNT DOWN	30
WOODLAND	32
THE BARRISTER WHO SUCKED HER THUMB	33
CHAPTER 4	**36**
THE CAT'S JOURNEY	36
THE FERRYBOAT	39
THE GREENHOUSE	41
PIGEONS IN THE LOFT	42
CHAPTER 5	**45**
THE GIRL WITH THE PEARL EARING	46
THE AVENUE OF TREES	47
THE PARALLEL UNIVERSE	48
THE POPPIES	50
MAN-TIDYING	51
CHAPTER 6	**53**
WHICH ME DO YOU WANT?	53
THE SIBANNAC TREE	54
THE SLAUGHTER IN BENTLEY PRIORY	56
THE PUB CRAWL	61
CHAPTER 7	**64**
DE BEAUVOIR SQUARE	64
THE LONELY MAN	68
THE GRAND OLD DUKE OF YORK	70
IN THE COUNTRY	71
THE VENDING MACHINE	73
CHAPTER 8	**75**
LOCKING THE DOOR AGAINST THE WORLD	75
THE RED BUTTON	77
THE BRIDGE	78

  SKYROCKETS 80
  MY ORNAMENTS 82
CHAPTER 9 84
  CHRISTINA'S WORLD 84
  MOBILE OBSESSION 85
  BRUSSELS 87
  THE PLANETS 88
  THE PLEASURES OF LIFE 89
CHAPTER 10 91
  THE PROMENADE DES ANGLAIS 91
  HERE LIES HENRY BLOOMFIELD 93
  A WALK THROUGH SARRATT 95
  AN AUTUMN STORY 95
  AUTUMN ARRIVES 97
  THOUGHTS 98
CHAPTER 11 100
  WEEDS IN THE GARDEN OF LIFE 100
  CUTTING DOWN THE TREE 101
  FLAMING KATY 103
  ROUTINE 103
  BOURNEMOUTH 105
  THE PLANET OF ODD SOCKS 107
CHAPTER 12 110
  URBAN CREATURES OF THE NIGHT 110
  THE ORIGINAL MEANING OF TWEET 111
  MYSTICAL 114
  AT PEACE IN NATURE 115
CHAPTER 13 117
  BOXES 117

    NATURE WORDS 119
    THE MAN AT THE TOP OF THE HILL................................. 120
CHAPTER 14 123
CHERYL'S ANTHOLOGY 123
    HANDICAPPED PEOPLE 126
    I AM A BUBBLE 126
    LOOKING IN A MIRROR 127
    THINKING.. 127
    OH WHAT SHALL I BE WHEN I GROW UP 128
    DECEMBER FROST 129
    APRIL WEATHER 130
    CLOUDS.. 130
    FRIENDSHIP 131
    JOY 132

Introduction

This book is an anthology of my poems, together with a selection of my paintings. It follows on from *Alone in the City*, published a few years before this. In addition, it contains a selection of the extensive work of poetry written by my late cousin, Cheryl Perlow. Detail about her life is contained in Chapter 14 of the book. However, at this juncture I would like to draw attention to the similarities and differences in Cheryl's and my style.

Cheryl was writing her poetry as a handicapped sixteen-year-old girl, and therefore displays an extremely brave acceptance of her situation, alongside charming naiveties reflecting her limited life experience. We both write about nature, and there are major similarities in that writing. But that's probably where the similarities end. If you want a cynical worldly-wise (albeit somewhat limited) view on life's experiences from a middle-aged man, read my poems.

This book is arranged in a different way to my last book. *Alone in the City* had subject headings within which I attempted to fit in my poems. This one has groups of five poems, each group starting off with a painting. I have attempted to include an amusing poem as the last one in each group; other than that there is no taxonomy. It is called *My Abstract Life*, so for the most part there are abstract paintings, which therefore cannot be associated with any poems. However, that is not always the case; I start with a representational painting, which does represent the subject matter of the first poem.

They say you should write about what you know. In many cases these poems are about things that happened to me or I observed; however in other cases they are about stories told to me, or I read about. I leave it to the reader to guess which is which. They are written over a period of about three years, whereas my first book was a collection of poems written over about fifteen years. Whether that has affected the quality is for the reader to judge.

Somebody once said to me, I believe in a sarcastic manner, "Oh, why don't you write a poem about it" referring to some everyday event. I say – why not? We can all write a poem a day about everyday mundane things that happen to us, such as in my poem in this book: My Day – A Saga. As a creative person I like either to write words or paint a picture; some things are easier done in one art form than the other. It is true that paintings give a person an immediate visual sensation, whereas poems take a bit more effort.

These poems are in simple rhyming verse. Don't ask me about any theoretical poetic constructs – I just find it easier to do my creative writing in simple verse. Just like my painting, I am untrained in poetic writing – I have got enough training to do for my day job!

Even if it is only my family that reads this book it doesn't matter. I feel a strong urge to create some sort of legacy. Other people procreate – I create paintings and books! If anybody other than family reads my books I consider that a big bonus.

My Abstract Life – isn't abstraction a step away from reality? Maybe that's the way I live my life, living in a dream world. However if that dreaming results in creative endeavours it's not a bad thing.

Paul Klinger
Stanmore, 2018

Chapter 1

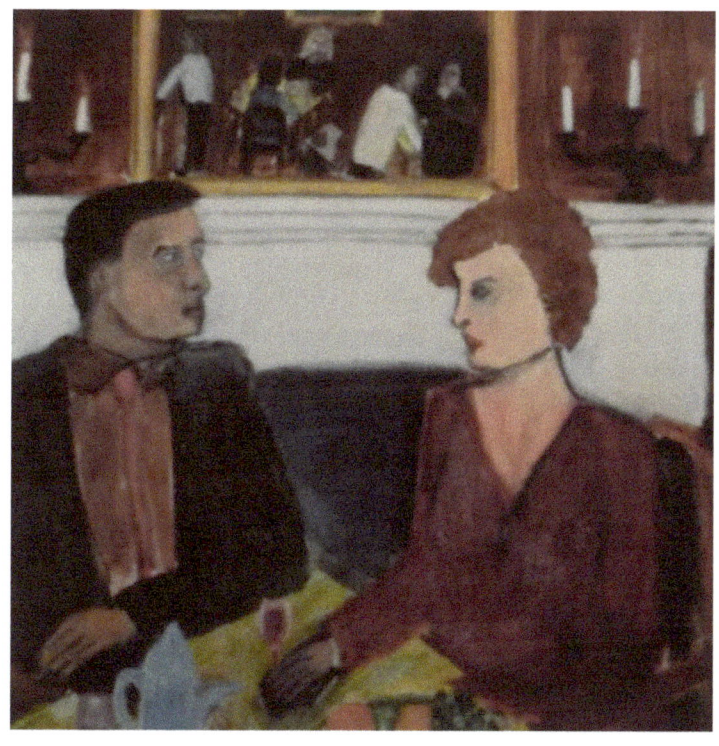

THE MAN AND WOMAN IN THE PICTURE

In the restaurant they sit
At the table, surrounded
By other couples, dumbfounded

At how their lives have turned out,
So that instead of a meal being enjoyed
They're working on plans to be employed

Discussing the future of their kids
And the breakdown of their marriages
And of births, deaths and miscarriages.

So much to discuss
And none of it uplifting
But it has to be aired, to stop them drifting

Further apart – think of the kids
They need a good education
So they can work for the good of the nation.

She still looks pretty, he's distinguished,
To an external observer, they're a good match,
And so they were, when their wedding was hatched.

But they slowly moved apart, due to
Work pressures, lovers and neuroses,
So one chapter begins after another closes.

In the same place where
Many years ago, sweet nothings were spoken
All that's left are their rings, a token.

And in the reflection of the mirror
On the wall of the restaurant,
They're not saying "I do", but "I can't".

IN THE SHADOW OF THE SHARD

In the shadow of the Shard
Sits a man who's living rough;
With his dog by his side,
He finds life is really tough.

Thirty floors above him
Lives a Saudi billionaire
Who got his money from oil
And he thinks that is quite fair.

In the shadow of the Gherkin
There's a two-up two-down.
Only one bedroom was used
So the resident's been kicked out of town.

By the local council who wanted
To let the extra room
To a banker who hadn't made
Enough money in the boom.

In the shadow of the Walkie-Talkie
A man sells the *Big Issue*
And people rush by
With busy lives to pursue.

Whilst way above, from a window,
An executive watches him.
Not seeing, just thinking
About his next visit to the gym.

In the shadow of Tower 42
Stands a man with mental issues.
You'd best look away
If he starts to stare at you.

Whilst many floors above
There's a banker, quite mentally stable
But who'd destroy the country for money
If only he was able.

In the shadow of City Hall
A pickpocket stalks his prey.
If he can get a mobile phone
It'll set him up for the day.

And on the floors above him
Stands Boris with his hair;
Working out how he can improve
What's going on down there.

PEOPLE

The clever one, the pretty one,
The tall one, the introvert.
The outgoing one, the shy one,
The saintly one, the pervert.

The sexy one, the handsome one,
The handy one, the academic.
The wise one, the silly one,
The loving one, the sceptic.

The business-like one, the smooth one,
The friendly one, the pessimist.
The serious one, the flippant one,
The unreliable one, the optimist.

The dreamy one, the jolly one,
The depressive one, the mystic.
The sickly one, the strong one,
The playful one, the artistic.

The little one, the big one,
The fat one, the life and soul.
The nervous one, the bold one,
The pale one, the one with a mole.

All these different people
All inhabiting the same space,
There's so many different types
Making up the human race.

THE CONCENTRIC CIRCLES

Concentric circles in the pond
As the water drops fall in the rain
Circles spreading outwards
Until another one comes again.

The single drop of water
Has an effect on all around
Like everything we do
The effect can be quite profound.

Circles of sorrow, circles of joy
Spreading out to those who are near
Circles of good, circles of evil
Causing wellbeing or maybe a tear.

The pond is like the whole world
Each raindrop is a person's feelings
The pond is a mixture of the different effects
Causing disease or sometimes healings.

Circles of poverty, circles of wealth
They both have an effect
Spreading to the areas around
To make worse or to correct.

Circles of ignorance, circles of wisdom
Subtracting or adding in their wake
Circles of love, circles of hate
Be careful which you make.

It's raining circles on the pond
Everything, everyone's affected
Make sure it's the right effect
And the bad things are corrected.

THE COUNTRY SQUIRE

There was a country squire
He was called Hilary Brampton-Groat.
He lived in a magnificent mansion
With fifty rooms and a moat.

He had a stately wife
She was the Lady Brampton-Groat.
She spoke with a plum in her mouth
And wore diamonds around her throat.

This magnificent upper class dame
Knew nothing of the squire's pastimes,
Chasing girls around the grounds
Between the oaks and between the limes.

He chased them round the maze
And into the horses' stable.
He could never remember their names –
Could have been Daisy, Joan or Mabel.

When his passion was really on fire
He went for the kitchen maid.
There was nothing she could do
If she wanted always to be paid.

He chased her into the garden
And round and round the parterre.
And if he was feeling daring
He'd kiss her mouth right there.

His favourites was a common girl,
He thought her name was Molly.
He made love to her when it was raining
In the classical Grecian folly.

He knew all the secret places
Where his wife would never go,
Such as the secret garden pergola
Or the circular glass gazebo.

Most of the girls were a bit saucy
And they didn't really mind.
They were used to randy aristocrats,
Who were all of a particular kind.

These naughty young wenches sighed
Remembering the words of their motto.
To keep their jobs it was necessary
To have the occasional fumble in the grotto.

But the squire of the Manor didn't know
Whilst he was having fun in the chamber-maid's room,
That the Honorary Lady Brampton-Groat
Was content in the arms of the groom.

Chapter 2

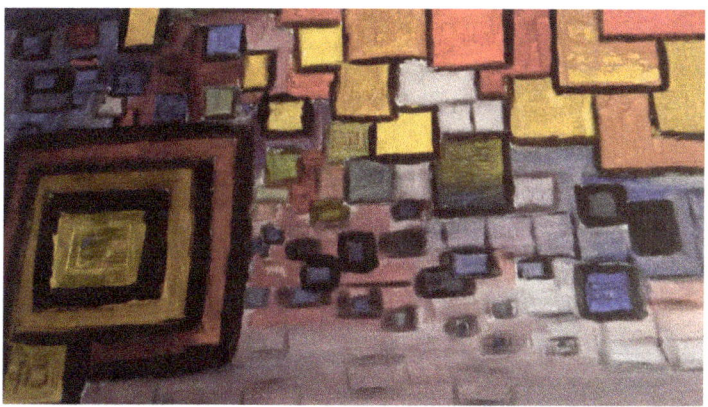

MY DAY – A SAGA

The alarm rings shrilly, the room is cold
The daylight has been overtaken by gloom.
I fight the sleep that drags me back to my dreams
Surrounded by the familiarity of my room.

I try to remember what day it is,
Is it a weekend or a working day?
Each has its disadvantages and benefits
Which I prefer – I cannot say.

I hit the button that says snooze, just a few minutes more
I think or say out loud.
Those few minutes turn into ten
Far more than I'm actually allowed.

And so the fight begins, the first of the day,
Battling to make up the time.
It's as if, if you're ten minutes late
You've committed some heinous crime.

I drag myself over to the scales
To check the effect of last night's meal,
I know I should do without potatoes
But hunger, it doesn't appeal.

Twelve stone and two pounds, ok
As long as it doesn't get any higher.
I've already gone up to a 36" waist
Don't want a 40 by when I retire.

I get my dressing gown, it feels nice and soft –
The first comfort of the day.
I get the feeling that by the time evening comes
I'm going to need plenty of comforts coming my way.

There'll be ups and there'll be downs, it's what life's about,
It may start off reasonably OK
But you can be sure that before it ends
Some bastard/s will ruin my day.

Driving to work

My car has to be reversed out of a shared drive
If the neighbour's van will allow.
I always manage to do it
But sometimes I wonder how.

There are so many parked cars
That I have constantly to give way
To drivers of vehicles
Who have no thank-you to say.

At the traffic lights two lanes merge
So that now there is only one.
The car behinds zooms in front
I think, shall I give two fingers or one?

But actually I'm a gentleman
And so of course I desist,
But inside I'm fuming like mad
And seeing much red mist.

It's normally a BMW
Or it could be man with a van
The sort that, if he approached you,
You'd better come up with a plan.

There are roadworks which have been promised,
By a yellow sign which declared with delight
That you'll be held up for a year, unless
You travel in the middle of the night.

I make up time on the motorway
Doing a speed at which I shouldn't go,
When a sign announces a slip-road queue
So you might as well reduce to slow.

So I realise there's no chance of attending
The meeting at half past nine
To discuss the quality aspects
Of a piece of software design.

And so my working day begins,
It's the first bad thing of the day.
I keep a tally in my head
Which I will eventually replay.

The working day

I creep up to my desk
Trying not to attract attention,
All the rest have been there since seven,
As to why, I have no comprehension.

It's now nine thirty, it's a disgrace
"Lazy sod," my colleagues probably think.
If they complained I'd cite flexitime
And probably kick up a stink.

If I've got no meetings it's boring
And it turns into a drag of a day.
But if I have, it means that I've got
To think of something intelligent to say.

I'm not part of a team
So nobody talks to me.
So I just get on with my work
And think of my salary.

It's an open plan office
With lots of noisy staff.
People shouting on the phone
Or having a very annoying laugh.

Which is very annoying for me
If I don't appreciate their jokes.
So I just admire the girls
And ignore the blokes.

I try to look out of the windows
Which seem a long way away,
But there are blinds drawn down
To block out the sun's rays.

And of course the windows don't open
So you can't get fresh air,
There's supposed to be air conditioning
But it might as well not be there.

I just dream of my lunch time break
When I'll be out for at least an hour,
Whether it's warm or whether it's cold
Whether it's sunny or there's a shower.

Lunch time

I eat my sandwiches at my desk
Pretending that I'm actually working,
It gives me a whole hour outside,
It's not really shirking.

When I go through the swing doors
And emerge into the fresh air
It's like breathing in nectar,
For a moment I don't have a care

Except to note the time
And clock out, later clock back in,
Mustn't defraud the company –
That's a sackable sin.

Once that's done I'm free
To walk round the park or the golf course,
Trying to dodge the golf balls
That they hit with such force.

I say hallo to the runners
Who pass me with a wave,
All of them colleagues,
Jack, John and Dave.

Or I might go into town
Seeing pretty things on the way,
Distracting me from my shopping –
A price I'm willing to pay.

I get back to my desk
If it's hot I'm in a sweat,
Hoping if somebody wants me
They won't come by just yet.

I read the news on my screen
It's the advantage of PCs,
Checking the disasters that happen
Hoping they don't affect me.

The afternoon

Staring at the screen
For five hours in the afternoon,
I have to pace myself because
I'm not going home anytime soon.

A tangerine after my lunch
A coffee at three p.m.
A walk round the car park at four,
If they object – stuff them!

Tea and a biscuit at five
Only an hour and a half to go.
By six I'm on the homeward straight,
It's very repetitive, I know.

But I think about the alternative
Sitting at home without any work.
At least in my job I have a title.
Home all day? I'd go berserk.

Principal Quality Engineer –
How grand does that sound?!
You'd think I'm the only one
But there are many more to be found.

At home I have no title,
I have no role in life.
I'm not the father of any children
Or the husband of any wife.

So it's best to keep on working
And the pay is pretty good,
Although I've always said
I'm earning less than I should.

At six thirty I pack up
And go to my trusty car
Which will take me back to London;
Twenty-five miles, not far.

The Evening

My Renault takes me home
Along the busy M1 motorway.
I've travelled along that route
More times than I can say.

On a Monday I stop off
To do my Sainsbury's shop.
I'm friendly with the staff
Because they see me such a lot.

I know Natalya from Russia
Who served me at the checkout.
She was pretty, with blonde hair
That made her stand out

From the mainly Asian women
Whose hair is always black.
But I was too friendly – now she's gone.
I seem to have the knack.

I make my evening meal
Listening to Coldplay on CD.
It's the best part of the day,
Doing things that relax me.

I speak to my partner on the phone
For an hour or sometimes more.
We live apart, it may seem strange
But we're better off I'm sure.

I watch the evening news
And wish I hadn't put it on,
If you took it all too seriously
You'd think the sun never shone.

Sometimes things seem routine
But I thank God for each day of good health.
And, believe it or not
I get reassurance from my bookshelf.

Because on there are my published books
Which nobody can take away,
As long as I'm creating, I need
To live for ten thousand days.

THE MISSIONARY COLLEGE

I stood in the deserted building,
Not a sound was to be heard,
Except for the howling wind outside
And the cry of some mysterious bird.

Long corridors stretched in four directions
Leading to myriads of rooms, like cells.
At one time these housed missionaries,
Studying, praying when summoned by the bells.

Learning, preparing to spread the word of God
In far-off nations across the globe.
In Africa, Asia, spreading Christianity's word
Dressed simply in their long plain robes.

This was a building full of good people
Who wanted nothing for themselves.
They wanted only to help others
To grow and to excel.

But now there was no need;
Christianity was doomed,
Along with other religions, except one
Within which the world will be subsumed.

So this building now stands empty.
I hear my footsteps echo
Past empty cells, empty rooms
Whichever way I go.

But then I come to the chapel
With its windows of coloured glass.
In here you can't hear the wind outside
But you get a sense of the past.

Biblical figures looking down on me
Looking right inside my soul.
I felt momentarily at peace;
I knew that I had a role

To play in this life,
Although uncertain of its meaning.
I understood how the missionaries came
To this building – there was a certain feeling.

As I left I looked back at the statue
Of St. Joseph with outstretched arm
Pointing towards Jerusalem,
In a way that was urgent, but calm.

I remembered seeing that statue
From my brother's room through the window
It can still be seen to this day
But like others, he had to go.

Maybe to the place indicated
By St. Joseph, showing the way;
The direction where I can meet him again
Some distant far-off day.

TRAVELLING ON THE TUBE

Sitting on the Jubilee line
On a day that's sunny and fine,
Opposite people in a row
None of whom you'll ever know.

Some of these hardy commuters
Stare into their tablet computers,
But what if you've no phone or book,
Where are you supposed to look?

There's a pretty girl with a short skirt
Not really intending to flirt.
But it's the sexiest thing to be seen
Between Stanmore and Willesden Green.

A man hiding behind his broadsheet paper
Imagines her on the escalator
All legs and high-heeled shoes –
It's better than reading the news.

There really isn't enough space
To fit his large… briefcase,
Because everybody now has backpacks
Sometimes coloured, sometimes black.

But if the backpack owner looks strange
Passenger glances may be exchanged.
They'll look at him with suspicion
Hoping there'll be no ignition.

Or, if anybody is a movie fan
They'll hope there's no criminal man
Who for hostages demands a fee
Like the *Taking of Pelham 1-2-3*.

But one will probably ascertain
That things are pretty mundane
And the most exciting event on the way
Is an announcement over the PA

By the driver who thinks he's a wit
But is actually a bit of a twit,
When he's explaining a short delay
With some humorous thing to say.

You can look for shapes on the Tube
But you'll never find any cube.
You'll definitely find a circle
Or a straight line that's coloured purple.

So if you've got no Kindle or book
And don't know where to look,
Examine the map, with many a line
And everything will turn out fine.

CELESTE

Her laughter was like the tinkle of a hundred little bells;
When she cried she wept tiny diamonds.
When she spoke her accent was cut-glass
She moved with the grace of a gazelle.

Her silky hair was the colour of gold,
Her skin was soft and pure.
Her cheekbones were high, her dimples cute;
You could not imagine her looking old.

Her fingers were long and slender
Her nails beautifully painted.
She never was angry, always calm
You knew her heart was tender.

She always married well, her husbands were rich
And always well connected.
Her weddings were sumptuous, well planned
Always happening without a hitch.

Her babies were born without any pain
And grew into beautiful children.
When you looked at her daughter you knew
That her beauty would be repeated again.

She was knowledgeable in fine art,
Paintings adorned the walls of her house.
She could talk about philosophy
From Plato to Descartes.

Her houses were sumptuous, furnished with taste,
Her dinner parties were social occasions
The food was haute cuisine.
Just enough, without any waste.

Oh beautiful Celeste, so perfect, well-bred
Is there anything that could be wrong?
If you wanted to discover that, take a look
At the thoughts going through her head.

BREAKFAST IN THE HOTEL

It's breakfast time in the hotel;
Service is a thing of the past.
It's self- service now
So you'd better not be last.

First get your cereal
And some fruit juice in addition,
And when you're ready for more,
Don't ask anyone's permission.

Get up to the hot food plates
Before anyone gets there first
And after a little while
You begin to notice your thirst.

But try to attract a waiter
To bring you a pot of tea –
It'll take you longer,
Than it takes to cross the North Sea.

Then you remember
You want a piece of toast.
For that you have to queue
If it's that you want the most.

That's when you have to be polite
And make pleasant conversation,
First thing in the morning
About the state of the nation.

When all you want to do
Is to keep yourself to yourself –
Not to enquire
About the state of some stranger's health.

And when you get back to your seat,
Guess what – your tea's disappeared.
Stolen by the waiter, who's greatest wish
Is to get your table cleared.

Bring back waiter service
Is what I truly say.
And then my morning breakfast
Will really set me up for the day.

CHAPTER 3

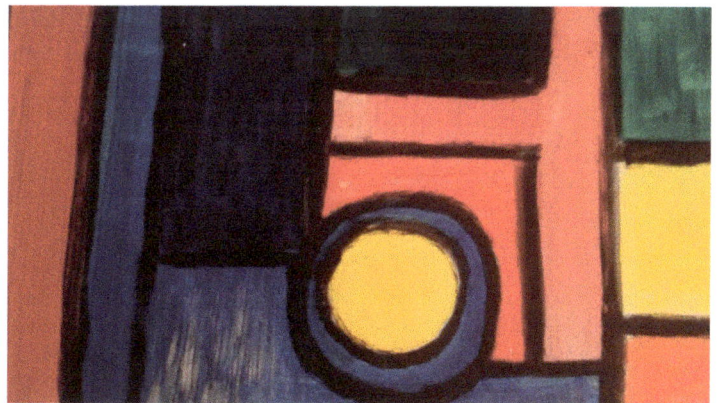

THE HORSE AND THE MAGPIE

There's an old folklore concerned with magpies that goes: "One for sorrow, two for joy, three for a girl, four for a boy...."

One fine day in a country field
In an Arcadian part of England's weald,
Stood two of God's creatures in deep conversation,
Speaking of fears, hopes and their many frustrations.

There was a magpie, saying to his friend, a horse:
"You served your time, now you've retired from the racecourse.
When you're not munching the grass, or your pile of hay,
How do you get through the rest of the day?"

The horse replied in plaintive tones:
"There are days when I feel creaking in my bones.
But my mind is still active, and I have many schemes
Running through my head, along many different themes."

"Humans don't realise I think in this way;
But even if they did, there's nothing I could say.
There's no way I can impart any information –
If I could, I'd speak without hesitation".

"Of course, I can communicate with you, a bird.
If only humans could have heard
The things we've talked about over the years –
They wouldn't be able to believe their ears!"

The magpie listened to these words;
He was a wily, cunning and thoughtful bird.
He thought for a while and then announced:
"I've thought of a plan to make your ideas count!"

"I want you to tell me what's in your head;
I can't write it down, but I'll remember it instead.
Tell me all the bits and pieces needed to realise your ideas
And I will collect (steal) all of those different wares".

So the magpie and the horse talked long into the night.
I'll not tell you about what – it wouldn't be right.
The bird committed all those things to memory,
Things that would seem complicated to you and me.

After a long while, the magpie decided
That enough information had been confided.
It thanked the horse for its intellectual endeavour
And said it'd be back soon, whatever the weather.

Over the next few days, the magpie worked hard
Obtaining objects from gardens, streets and a yard.
It got everything required to put into place
The horse's plan to improve the human race.

But it was not able to carry out any construction.
You may think that that would be an obstruction.
Not at all, that is where this cunning bird
Played on superstitions that you may have heard.

It identified people who would be extremely good
At making things, out of glass, metal and wood.
Both the magpie and its wife would suddenly appear
In front of these people, together, paired.

Whoever had put objects together in a way that looked about right;
Which were approximately the right width, depth and height
These people were rewarded, and shouted, "Magpies, and two for joy!"
But really they had fallen for our friend's ploy.

But if people had done nothing with the bits,
Or if they assembled things which didn't really fit,
The magpie would appear singly, on its own
And the people would do the things, which were well known:

They would bow down, saying: "Good day Mr. Magpie, how's your wife?"
It's necessary to do this to avoid any strife.
If this happened on more than one occasion
They'd put two and two together, an equation.

They'd realise that to get not one magpie but two
There were things it was necessary to do;
Assembling things to satisfy the Plan –
This was eventually done, by each and every man.

So in this way the magpie got things done.
It took a long time, but eventually the battle was won.
The same principle was used for people in power
Who sat in their palaces, mansions and towers.

To get people to use what had been designed by the horse
And made by the people who the magpie had forced
By dint of tradition and old folklore
It pushed the horse's ideas more and more.

So that eventually these things were in everyday use.
These were common sense ideas, not abstruse.
And who would have thought they'd been designed
By a retired racehorse, who to the field had been consigned.

So the next time you see a bird close to a horse,
Just listen closely, and you'll hear a discourse
From which something brilliant could arise –
Something only a horse and a magpie could devise.

FROM MY HOTEL WINDOW

I see the sea, restless, never still.
I see the green grass on Polruan Hill.
(And my Scotch glass needs a refill).
From my hotel window.

I see the yachts bobbing up and down.
I see the Polruan houses, some white, some brown.
(But a dark thought makes me frown).
From my hotel window.

I see the trees on the far shore.
I see where the water taxis moor.
(But there are no big freighters any more).
From my hotel window.

I see the woods through which I walked.
I hear snippets of speech that is talked.
Reflections from boat windows are caught.
From my hotel window.

I see sunlit clouds in a windy sky.
I see gulls and birds go wheeling by,
(People in this hotel think I'm shy).
From my hotel window.

I see people walking by looking into my room.
I see them wondering what I'm writing and to whom.
(I wish they'd stop looking in my room).
From my hotel window.

I see Victorian street lamps lighting up too soon.
I see the waves and hear their soulful tune,
As they wait for the rising of the moon.
From my hotel window.

I see people who think: "he's on his own!"
I see people wanting to know why I'm alone.
(It's none of their business, if the truth be known).
From my hotel window.

THE DAY THE PIER BURNT DOWN

The Middle East was in turmoil
There was trouble in Ukraine,
We were having a hot summer
With hardly any rain.
The day the pier burnt down.

There was a new disease in Africa
The TV showed faces in pain.
The economy was in trouble
With interest rates down again.
The day the pier burnt down.

None of that meant anything to me,
I had only one memory –
Of the pier stretching out to the sea.

The Cold War was restarting
Immigration was in the news.
I didn't like the news from Europe
With so many far-right views.
The day the pier burnt down.

Scotland tried to be independent
There were the Commonwealth Games.
World crises were confusing
You didn't know who to blame.
The day the pier burnt down.

But I just remember strolling
With my arm around my first love,
Out on the pier, above the waves that were rolling.

The Conservatives were worried
UKIP was winning at the polls.
The Tories were trying to appeal
To people who didn't own a Rolls.
The day the pier burnt down.

The Army was half the strength
Than it once used to be,
But unless there was a war
It didn't matter to me.
The day the pier burnt down.

I just want it rebuilt with fresh planks of wood
So I can stroll with my beloved,
Whispering the things that I should.

WOODLAND

"Private woodland, no public access," it said on the notice, pinned to the gate. It made me wonder what went in those private woods…

What do they do in their private woods?
Do they hug the trees to make themselves feel good?
Do they climb the trunks and sit in the boughs,
Watching the horses, the sheep and the cows?

Do they have wild parties, with plenty of sex,
Which you can't find out about by phone or by text?
Do they drink strong alcohol in copious amounts,
Drinking more units than they could possibly count?

Do they take off their clothes and dance in the nude,
Which would certainly not suit if you're a bit of a prude?
Is there a witches' coven amongst the tall oaks
Where they conjure up spells to spook all the folks?

Are they growing cannabis or some other weed,
Providing more highs than they possibly could need?
Are they testing out some secret radio waves;
Are they storing something nasty in dank, dark caves?

And what happens when day turns to night –
If you trespass then you won't be alright.
The next morning when people look for you
All they'll find is a hat and a shoe.

Nobody will know what terrors you faced
As you looked around and quickened your pace.
As branches brushed you and hands reached out
And the howling winds muffled your shout.

As the breath of the devil breathed down your neck.
As your heart missed a beat and your breathing was checked.
Before what was you became just a hot sticky mess,
You'll remember the words "Private, no access!".

THE BARRISTER WHO SUCKED HER THUMB

There was a lady barrister
Well known in the Inns of Court,
From Lincolns Inn to Inner Temple
Her services were sought.

She excelled as a criminal barrister,
Words tripped off her tongue
She could silence the opposition
Even from when she was young.

She never learnt her briefs,
She relied on her acid wit.
If defence counsel argued
She'd come back with a hit.

But she had one big weakness
Which seemed very bizarre to some;
Because this lady barrister
Loved to suck her thumb.

She sucked it in front of the jury,
She sucked it in front of the judge.
It was one of those childhood habits
That stubbornly refused to budge.

One day there was a cockney defendant,
Time for his cross-examination had come
So he stood up and exclaimed:
" 'Ere, that barrister's sucking her thumb!"

The ladies and gentlemen of the jury,
The judge, and the public as well,
Turned to look at the barrister,
And as far as was possible to tell

Yes, she was sucking her thumb,
And the judge's eyebrows were raised.
He addressed the lady barrister
Saying: "I really am amazed."

"That a pillar of the Establishment
In such a learned profession
Should practise a childhood habit
When this crown court is in session".

But the lady barrister said
To the judge sitting in his high seat
"Your Honour, it helps me concentrate,
When I'm thinking on my feet".

"And if justice is to be done
In this very important place
I'll continue to suck my thumb –
It's got such a very nice taste!"

So the criminal justice system,
Which is normally so humdrum,
Was enlivened when learned counsel
Was the barrister who sucked her thumb.

CHAPTER 4

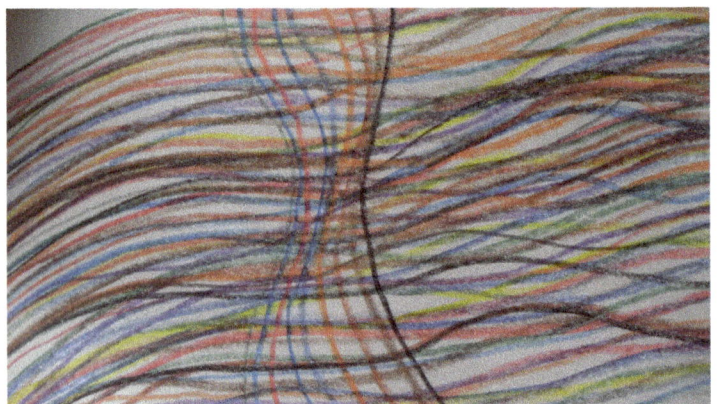

THE CAT'S JOURNEY

Everyday we have our human life,
Everyday our cat has its cat's life,
Two lives coming together, meeting, during the day
But at night, who can say?

On a quiet starry night
The cat sets out on its journey.
A journey about which no human knows,
Along streets and between hedgerows.

Come with it on its journey
And together you, and this wise creature
Will discover mysteries of the night
That don't happen during daylight.

It leaves its house stealthily
Creeping out through the cat flap.
Its owners sleep soundly on
Dreaming about the day just gone.

It stalks down the garden path
Alert to sounds and smells.
It heightens its senses
As it creeps past the garden fences.

It slinks past a car park
Where a single car stands alone.
There's a lovers' tryst inside
As the cat walks silently beside.

It moves on to the high street, now silent
Except for dark figures outside the bank.
The cat senses evil intentions
But cannot offer intervention.

So it moves on through the street,
Past an occupied shop doorway.
A down-and-out, almost sleeping
Strokes it for a greeting.

The cat miaows in return, and continues
Until the high street reaches its end.
It carries on until a field
To see what it will yield.

It hopes to find field mice
Or other animals for some sport,
But they've been given notice to quickly flee
By an owl watching from high in a tree.

There's a noise in the bushes
As a fox comes slinking through.
The two creatures look at each other
Having an understanding, like sister and brother.

The cat looks up into the heavens
Seeing planets and shooting stars
And other wondrous things in the sky,
But has no need to ask why.

Something white floats by
Something spectral, unseen.
The cat's ears prick up, it sniffs
As into the air the ghost lifts.

These things the cat sees,
These things the cat can't tell.
Mysteries it will keep
From up high and down deep.

As the moon shines down on the cat
It sees mysterious dancing spirits.
It sees fairies, elves and gnomes
In the gardens outside people's homes.

It sees things humans can't see,
Of which we know nothing.
You can watch its head turning
To watch some spirit, returning.

The cat creeps back to its owners' home
And falls asleep beside the fire.
In the morning it will be stroked
But nothing can invoke

The mysteries of the night gone by,
Or the adventures remaining untold.
The cat lies there silent, except for a purr.
All it has seen stays inside, trapped by the fur.

THE FERRYBOAT

The ferryboat made its way
Across the gently lapping waves,
Past yachts bobbing in greeting –
There was a generally calm feeling.

After last night's storms
When the ferryman wouldn't cross,
When the river was harsh and rough,
The ferryman wasn't that tough.

I had to stay this side of the river,
Even though I wanted to cross
To be where the fairy lights were twinkling;
Instead I had to sit here drinking

From my glass of Scotch whisky,
Which was a comforting substitute
For not being under the fairy lights
Which shone so bright last night.

Last night, when the wind blew hard,
When the trees bent over
And the windows rattled
Joining in the battle.

When the lighthouse flashed
Its bright urgent warning:
Don't go out to sea;
Please, obey me!

Last night, when the Town Quay was flooded
And there were sand bags against the houses.
Because the flood was due
And the people knew

The ways of the river;
They knew what the river would do –
When it would be angry, when it would be calm,
So nobody came to any harm.

And now the sun is setting
On my last night in Fowey.
I see a flock of birds in a line;
Their intent is the same as mine.

Returning to their home;
But they'll be back another day.
Humans and birds, returning to the sea
Because it's where we want to be.

THE GREENHOUSE

In our garden there was a greenhouse
It was where we used to play.
Sometimes it was a boat
On choppy seas, afloat.

And sometimes it was a train;
I was the driver at the front
With my brother sitting behind me,
We were happy kids, we were free

To let our imagination run riot.
That greenhouse could be anything:
One day a boat, one day a plane,
No two days ever the same.

We didn't think of its real use
Where things should grow in pots.
That was for our parents to do
For reasons only they knew.

We had better ideas, us kids
And when we shut that door
We could forget all about our homework
And pretend we were Captain Kirk.

On the Starship Enterprise
Travelling through outer space;
The fact that it was broad daylight
Didn't make it any less right.

The greenhouse has been knocked down
But the base is still standing there.
Listen – on a day that's sunny and bright
You'll still hear our shouts of delight.

PIGEONS IN THE LOFT

In deepest darkest Lowestoft
There's a man who lives in a loft.
He shares his loft with a pigeon
Which has no specific religion.
Apparently this pigeon is a genius
But the man thinks this is erroneous
Because if it was such a clever bird
It should be ok with the *Times* crossword.

But the man put the pigeon to the test
And asked him to do his best.
But when it came to twenty-three down
The pigeon gave a small frown,
It was a very cryptic clue
To do with the price of glue
So they put the crossword away
To try it on another day.

Anyhow, because it was boring in the loft
In deepest darkest Lowestoft
The man thought he'd try a joint
He knew it wouldn't disappoint.
He imagined he was in Ealing,
With an orange that he was peeling
Then he thought he'd go disguised
But that was the start of his demise.

He became very pensive
About a car that was too expensive,
But because of his cunning disguise
He had what looked like lady's eyes.
The salesman got quite turned on
And he bought it for a song
Now he finds his loft too boring
So he goes to a place called Goring.

Meanwhile, the pigeon, who was single
Gradually began to mingle
With a girl pigeon who was charming
And had a penchant for ten-pin bowling.
But it was difficult to hold the balls
So they went and perched on some walls.
She was a very good catch
Because soon a baby was hatched.

Meanwhile, the man, known as Jake
Decided to bake a cake,
Because he'd been watching too much telly
And was obsessed with Mary Berry.
The pigeons, now a family group
Decided that, after soup
Cake was the next best thing
If you wanted to live like a king.

So they headed back to the loft
In deepest darkest Lowestoft.
They didn't want to forsake
The man we now know as Jake,
So all four, the man and the birds,
Although it was a bit absurd
Have jolly good loft parties
With cakes which are full of Smarties.

There's not much more I can say
They're still happy to this day.
The baby pigeon, who learnt to do crosswords
Entered a competition, and came third.
The man dresses as a girl
Known by the name of Pearl
They're all happy in their loft
In deepest darkest Lowestoft.

CHAPTER 5

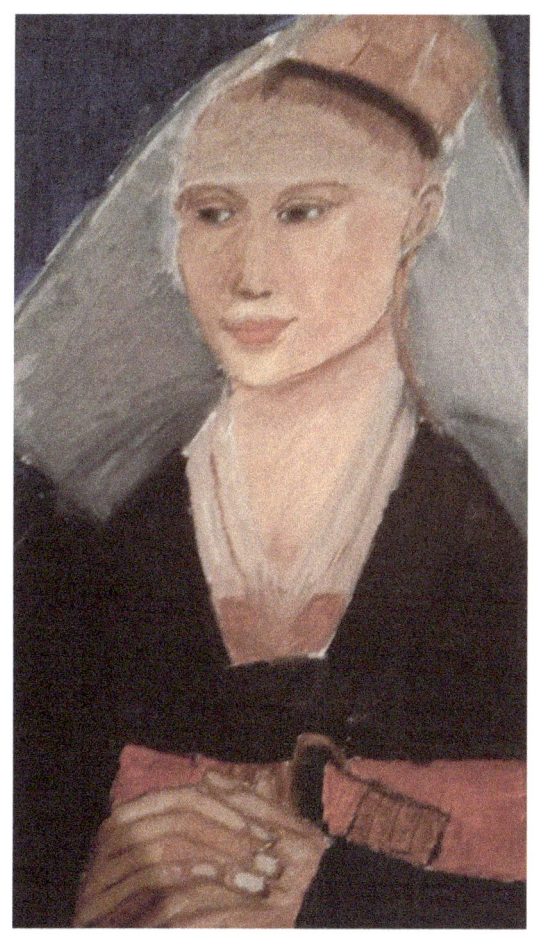

THE GIRL WITH THE PEARL EARING

I painted the girl
Before I saw the film.
So whatever she's wearing
I'm afraid there's no pearl earing.

And it's not a copy of a Vermeer
On which I think the film was based.
The original was by Van de Weyden
Who spotted this pretty maiden.

I'm sorry if you haven't seen the film.
I can't remember who produced it.
But the actress was Johannsen, Scarlet
A twenty-first century starlet.

She's at the top of my stairs
(The picture, that is; I wish it was Scarlet).
As I ascend she's watching me
With an air of superiority.

Which I gave her, when I painted her;
Yes, she was my creation.
That's the joy of art –
When you create you impart

A life, from something lifeless.
And it will last, as a legacy.
Even when I'm not around
It might continue to astound.

But I'm being vain, I'm an amateur,
Although I hope I've done some good stuff.
Looking at your own creation, said Churchill
Always gives you a thrill.

The Girl Without the Pear Earing
Is definitely one of my best.
I hope you'll enjoy looking at this girl
Who longs for an earing, with a pearl.

THE AVENUE OF TREES

I have walked through this avenue of trees
For more than thirty years
I hear snippets of people's conversations –
Their joys, their hopes their fears.

Always with good accents, because it's Hampstead;
Some may say: a privileged class.
They may have got off to a good start,
But how long will it last?

Sometimes I hear a foreign language
But normally it's my mother tongue,
Spoken by people of all ages
But often quite young.

Discussing with their friends
What life is throwing at them,
And wondering what new experiences they'll get
From Monday morning nine a.m.

Those trees absorb it all –
It's embedded in their bark.
Just like the rings in their trunks
Those words must leave their mark.

One day there'll be a way
To playback all those words;
The laughter and the speech
And all else that was heard.

Just like those initials
Carved into the trees with a knife,
There'll be a record of friends and lovers
In many a person's life.

Be careful what you say
When you go on your Hampstead walk;
It's not just me that can hear
Every word that you talk.

THE PARALLEL UNIVERSE

There's a parallel universe by your side
You can't see it because it can easily hide.
It's like our world, but the constants have changed.
Subtle things, but it's enough to rearrange

Things such that in it we couldn't survive,
It would be no good to us if we were alive.
But what about the people no longer with us – dead;
They may be dead in our universe, but there's another instead,

Where loved ones can survive, existing next to you,
Joining in all the daily things that you do.
It's the answer to, "where do people go"?
The answer is, "not far," if you really want to know.

The parallel universe has more dimensions than three.
This is what quantum physicists have told me.
But this was known many centuries ago
By Kaballists, who were in the know.

This explains the feelings of déjà vu,
Things that seem familiar to you.
And another thing – when people die their atoms don't;
When it rains maybe their buried atoms float,

And get back to that parallel place
Which occurs next to the human race
By means of evaporation into the air.
Or by the meat from animals grazing there.

Our souls may in fact be electromagnetic fields
Absorbed into the parallel universe, which yields
A person very similar to us,
But different because something is minus instead of plus.

It's nice to think that loved ones may not have gone,
So now you know what's meant by, "they've passed on".
It's just that a few of the parameters are new,
So don't worry, they're not far from you.

THE POPPIES

They told me to go to see the red poppies
That had been spread over London Town,
To celebrate an important centenary –
It made perfect sense to me

To try to find the red poppies
Wherever they had been placed;
I didn't know their location
But I made it my vocation

To search all over my home town,
And to share with my fellow citizens
What was once patriotic pride,
Which these days you have to hide.

There were no poppies in Trafalgar Square
And none along Northumberland Avenue.
The Victoria Embankment had nothing in red
Although there were girls in dark cloaks instead.

They were going to a masked ball
Held under Waterloo Bridge's arches.
There were hundreds queuing to get in –
All tall, pretty and thin.

I dragged my eyes away from this sight
And continued my search for the flowers.
There were none around the Egyptian Obelisk –
I checked, I could confirm this.

I searched all over Waterloo Bridge;
I mingled with people on the South Bank.
I looked around the Festival Hall
And around the OXO tower, standing so tall.

There was nothing at Blackfriars Bridge,
Nothing around the cathedral at St. Pauls,
No poppies were in Upper Thames Street,
Although there were plenty of people to meet.

I passed Billingsgate market
The fish market had long gone.
There were no fish to be seen.
And the buildings had been given a clean.

And then I saw them – a swathe of red
In the moat encircling the Tower.
My search had a last been fruitful,
And the poppies – they were plentiful.

As a token to those who had died
In all the brutal wars.
They'd be there until Remembrance Sunday....
And forgotten by the following Monday.

MAN-TIDYING

There are crumbs on my carpet
And I think they need a vacuum,
But I've got a poem in my head
More important than my back room.

The shelves need dusting,
But there's a picture I want to paint.
It only seems dusty when the sun shines
So you'll have to exercise restraint.

The bathroom floor needs a clean,
It just needs a bit of a mop,
But if I don't get this idea down
My next novel will be a flop.

The garden lawn needs mowing
And I've seen another weed,
But I've bought a new book
That I'm just aching to read.

The kitchen sink's got a stain
And the cupboards need a wipe,
But there's an article for a magazine
I really have to type.

There are papers lying around
Which should really be put away.
But I've come to the conclusion
It can wait for another day.

CHAPTER 6

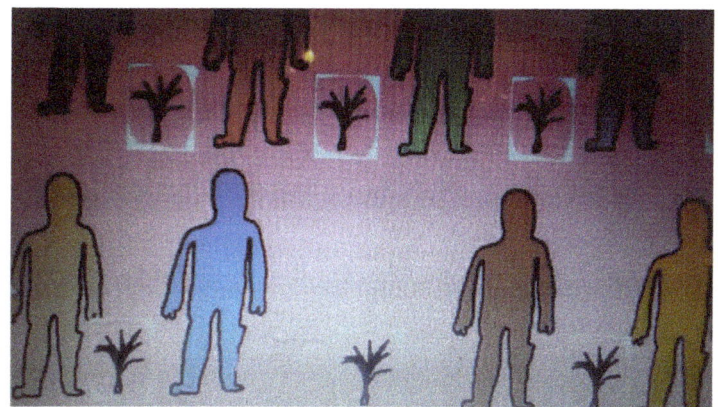

WHICH ME DO YOU WANT?

The telephone rings. "Is that Mr...?"
"Well, that depends, which version of me do you want?"

Do you want the me that is my partner's partner,
Or the me that is my mother's son?
She had two before
But now she's got just the one.

Do you want the me that is my nieces' uncle
Or the me that my friend's friend?
It used to be friends, plural
But that came to an end.

Do you want the me that is my colleagues' colleague,
Or the me that people pass in the street?
Who in England just pass on by
But in other countries I'd greet.

Do you want me that is my aunt's nephew,
Or me that's my cousins' cousin?
If you count the once-removed
I've probably got a dozen.

Do you want me that's educated and intelligent,
Or the me that cocks up yet again?
The first you won't see much of
But the second's a daily refrain.

Do you want the me that's sweet and gentle,
Or the me with the nasty streak?
Well, that depends on the things that you do
And the words that you speak.

THE SIBANNAC TREE

The sibannac tree looks inviting
With its leaves of a golden hue.
Don't pluck the leaves of the Sibannac tree
If you know what's good for you.

If you pluck the leaves of the Sibannac tree
And breathe in their glorious scent
You'll find you'll be saying "Ollah"
When it's "hallo" that you meant.

You'll find that when you look up
Hoping to see the blue of the sky,
You'll be seeing fields of green
Where plants and stones can lie.

When you try to read a book
Hoping to read from left to right,
You'll find sentences start the other way
Maybe there's something wrong with your sight?

If you've been born on the first of April
In nineteen eighty-one,
You'll discover you've aged forty years
If you say that date to someone.

If you're a teacher in a school, please don't
Call the register of names,
Because you'll find you start with Zoe
And call Adam after James.

When you read your newspaper, I hope
That you really enjoy your sport,
Because it's the first thing that you'll read
Even if it's headlines you sought.

When you're driving on the motorway
I hope there are no other cars,
Because you'll be driving fast in the slow lane
Even when you've not visited bars.

You'll go through the front door to your garden
And your backdoor to the street,
And you'll wonder in your garden
Why there are no people there to greet.

You'll put on your trousers first
And then your underpants on top.
You'll wonder why you're getting funny looks
When you go into that shop.

I told you to keep well clear
Of that wondrous Sibannac tree
But no, you didn't listen;
You took no notice of *'em!*

THE SLAUGHTER IN BENTLEY PRIORY

I passed a girl in Bentley Priory
She was pretty, and she said hello.
We spoke of the nice afternoon
And I was just about to go.

But she came back towards me
She seemed to want some conversation,
I thought that was good
And an unusual situation.

But it was for a good reason
And that reason was not to do with me,
Her dogs had lagged behind
And were not where they ought to be.

There was a large Alsatian
Within the deer park enclosure.
I said to the girl, is he stuck?
Maybe we should help him over.

She said that no,
He belonged to one of the big houses, so grand.
The deer park was private
And was part of their extensive land.

And then she told me a story
Those made my very flesh creep.
The sort of story that disturbs,
And stops you from getting to sleep.

She told of a day, last week
When she was taking her dogs for a walk
There was a man in the deer enclosure
Who didn't look like he wanted to talk.

He was rounding up the deer
The stags and the little ones too.
He was driving them up to the big house
Away from the public view.

A few minutes later she was walking
Where there would normally be grazing deer.
She heard a shot ring out,
And an animal's cry of fear.

And then another shot, and another
And an eerie silence pervaded.
The terror inside her increased
As the life of each deer faded.

She grabbed her dogs
And ran, as fast as she could
Past fields and bushes
Up the path through the woods.

It seemed to her the trees were crying
And the stream carried away their tears.
Then everything fell silent
There was not even birdsong to hear.

The people in the big house had decided
That there had been too many deer breeding,
So it was necessary to carry out a cull
Which would involve a lot of shooting.

The girls said, "how did they decide
Which would live and which would die?
If they killed the little ones
You have to ask yourself why"

Those little ones, the Bambis
It was their home, their safe land.
And just a day earlier, they
Were feeding from children's hands.

You cannot tell the children
Can you imagine how they would feel,
They wouldn't believe adults could be so cruel
Or could do something so unreal.

I cannot feel the same
Now when I walk through the Priory,
I feel a sadness and an anger
Welling up inside me.

How could they do such a thing
To creatures so innocent and cute,
Who looked into the face of a man
Who was preparing to shoot?

But then I remembered I ate meat
So who was I to talk?
I have all of these thoughts
Everytime I take that walk.

And if I meet that girl
Again on one bright sunny day
I'll have plenty of thoughts to share
Plenty of sad things to say.

THE MOTORWAY

Tankers, cars and vans,
Articulated lorries of all kinds
Making their way up North
Following the big blue signs.

Breakdown trucks towing;
Now the traffic is slowing.
Is there something wrong?
We'll find out before long.

Lots of bright coaches
Carrying people to different towns.
I wonder what they're thinking about
As they abstractly gaze down?

They've got their headphones on
Probably listening to some song.
It's a hell of a long way there
But, hey, they got a cheap fare.

Police cars zooming past,
Their blue lights flash.
On the trail of some criminal
Who's escaped with the cash.

Seventy miles an hour, eighty,
I've been going a bit fast lately.
Should slow down to the limit
But that's a bit boring, innit!

It's good to spot the lorries
From all those different firms.
You get to know the names,
There's always a new one to learn.

Stobart, they always have two girls' names –
There are never two exactly the same.
There's Fowler Welch, and DHL,
Primark and Argos have trucks as well.

There are lorries from Poland,
Lorries from Spain,
And lorries from Slovakia
That have travelled through the rain.

They're all left-hand drive,
The driver's on the other side.
So you'd better be sure when you pass
That he can see you in the mirror's glass.

When I see the big trucks
I remember my Dinky Toys
And I want to play with them
Just like when I was a boy.

But I'm trying to concentrate
So I don't make a mistake;
Keeping my eye on the road,
Not on a lorry's load.

Oh well, here's Junction Ten,
And I hope I get a chance
To leave the motorway just here
If I can get past that truck from France.

THE PUB CRAWL

I started at the Hope and Anchor
Downing a beer at a leisurely pace.
This was going to be a long evening
So I could drink slowly, without haste.

I moved on to the Dog and Duck
Where I met a man from the press.
I said, "Do you do phone hacking?"
And he said, "Oh, yes!!"

In the Olde Bull and Bush I met a politician
I asked him, was he Labour, Conservative or LibDem.
I think he was slightly drunk
Because he answered "All of dem!!"

Soon I was in the Wells Tavern
Drinking deep from my Holsten Pils.
It was definitely having an effect
Because I stopped worrying about my bills.

By now I was in my stride
So I headed for the Cat and Fiddle.
Don't ask me how I got there
Because that was quite a riddle.

Next was the King of Bohemia.
In there I met an actress.
I asked her whether she was famous.
She said no, but did I like her dress?

I thought I was doing alright,
But I lost her on the way to the Queen's Head.
I thought, "there's plenty of fish in the sea.
I'll find someone else instead".

Next up was the Flask
Where I met a man from Peru.
I tried to start up a conversation
But he just asked me the way to the loo.

I staggered into the Fighting Cocks
I asked for a pint of London Pride.
When they charged me four-fifty
I thought, "I'm being taken for a ride".

So I retired to the Hare and Hounds
Where I met a man who'd been in jail.
When he told me what he'd done
It made me go all pale.

So I headed straight for the Bricklayer's Arms
And sat down on a comfortable bench.
I didn't sit there for long because I saw
That the barmaid was a busty wench.

As I walked into the Three Horseshoes
I saw a neighbour from when I lived nearby,
He saw me and the next thing I knew
He was saying his goodbyes.

That made me quite upset
So I headed for the Five Bells
And sat in the corner drinking
And eating my peanuts in shells.

By the time I got to the Vine
Nothing seemed to be very clear.
So I asked the barman for a taxi
And got charged an exorbitant fare.

The next day I passed the Bald Faced Stag
And my mind was still all of a fog.
But, I thought, the best thing to do
Would be to go in for the hair of a dog.

CHAPTER 7

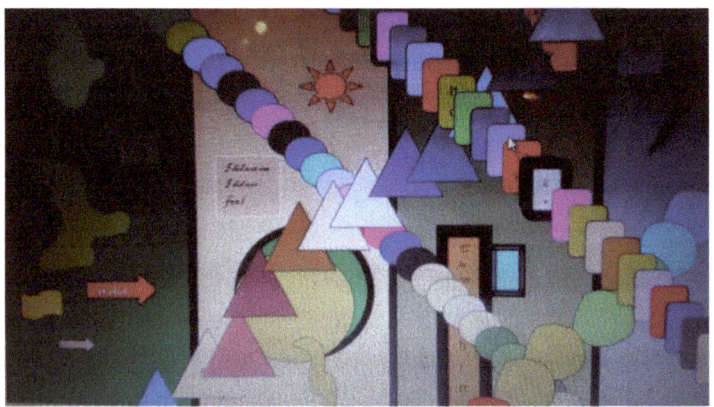

DE BEAUVOIR SQUARE

I stood opposite the block of flats
In leafy De Beauvoir Square,
I watched as a woman emerged
From the elegant doorway there.

I wondered if there were times
When she was lying awake
Could she smell the oil of the machines,
Or the noises they would make?

Could she hear the lively voices
Of the happy women, never cross.
Because they had no hard taskmaster
Only my father, the boss.

Did she ever see him
Carrying his heavy load
Unaided, from the lorry
That was parked out in the road?

Unloading cardboard for the machines
To be made into boxes of different sizes,
Which would end up as presents
For birthdays, weddings, or surprises.

There stood his factory, where the flats are now.
It provided work for local people
And didn't look unsightly
Near the church with the big steeple.

Making boxes for perfumes, boxes for dolls
With colourful labels, with different patterns
And when you looked inside
There was a blanket of satin.

Boxes for after-shave, boxes for soap,
Boxes for record sets, classical and pop.
Sometimes you could see our boxes
In the high street shops.

Sometimes he brought work home
And my mother and I would sit
Threading satin through cardboard,
Making sure of a nice fit.

I sometimes got half a crown
For my efforts – I was only young
And it was satisfying and creative
To see the way the satin hung.

Everything was done by my father
The design, manufacture and sales.
The heavy work, the paper work
He could not possibly fail.

And when the machines broke down
He had his box of bits.
He didn't call out an engineer
If he had something that fits.

Sometimes it was a bit Heath Robinson
And wouldn't pass Health and Safety,
But in those days there was nothing like that
Affecting him, the workers, or me.

He employed ten women,
When I was there I was very shy
Amongst all those jolly ladies
Who sometimes gave me the eye.

There was one girl I remember
Not much older than me, young;
And I loved the special smile I got
Reserved for the boss's son.

My father would be there
At eight thirty, rain or shine
To open the doors for the women
So they clocked in on time.

It was a family concern, my father and my uncle
So Klinger Boxes was its name.
Maybe if his sons had joined it would still be there
Still be in the boxes game.

My brother wasn't interested, and he didn't want me in it,
Said that in that business there was no future
So I studied electronics
And how to program a computer.

The competition was tough
Amongst companies that much bigger,
And when the lease ran out
My father had to consider

Whether it was worth continuing
Or should he close the business down
And that's just what he did
In leafy De Beauvoir Town.

It used to be called Dalston,
But it's come up, gentrified.
Houses there a worth probably a million
You could get that if you tried

To sell land in that area
But the factory was not owned, it was leased,
So he got nothing when it closed
Except some inner peace.

Because he wasn't then responsible
For the wages and welfare
Of the ten or more women
Who spent their working days there.

But he didn't stop work, at sixty
He became a consultant on pensions
Earning a good living
Without responsibility or tension.

So the factory was knocked down
And Klinger Boxes no longer existed
But you can't take memories away –
They always persisted.

I remember the work he did
When I see soap nicely presented,
In a lovely little box
With coloured satin inserted.

Like the satin lovingly put in
As carefully as we were able
Cosy in our house,
On our dining room table.

THE LONELY MAN

He sat there in the restaurant
Alone, facing the wall.
Everyone else was talking, happy
But he studiously avoided them all.

His shoulders hunched, concentrating
On his meal of fish and chips,
He got the waitress to bring a doggy bag
And left without paying a tip.

Head down, scurrying
Away like a hated rat.
Back, no doubt, to the squalor
Of an untidy, unkempt flat.

No woman to look after him,
Nobody sees the mess inside;
Papers, boxes, rubbish
That he doesn't bother to hide.

He turns on the TV, whatever is on;
It something just to look at.
He strokes his only companion,
A mangy, scruffy little cat.

He goes to bed unaccompanied
Between sheets dirty and torn
Dreams of girls help him sleep
Right through to the breaking dawn.

Then he gets up and goes out
To his job of sweeping the streets.
Plenty of people pass him
But there's no-one for him to meet.

He dated when he was younger
But girls weren't very impressed,
So he withdrew, and became bitter
And about some things, obsessed.

Existing from day to day,
Keeping on the right side of the law
Doing what he can to survive,
Nothing less, nothing more.

He's past caring now
Nothing's going to change.
He's too set in his ways
For his life to be rearranged.

But there's one thing to look forward to –
That weekly visit for a meal.
If you sit next to him, don't try to converse
Because he really won't appeal.

THE GRAND OLD DUKE OF YORK

The Grand Old Duke of York
He had Ten Thousand Men
He marched them up to the top of the Hill
And marched them down again.

And when he returned to his grounds
His parade was nowhere to be found.
What did he find instead?
Tracy Emin's unmade bed.

In front of his buildings so grand,
Where once was his marching band,
The Saatchi Gallery now stood
Exhibiting mouldy lumps of wood.

Instead of reveille at dawn
Were pictures some call porn.
Instead of soldiers of rank
There was a pickled shark in a tank.

When the uniforms needed washing a lot
To get rid of unsightly spots,
They had to check whether they'd be useful first
To the artist Damian Hirst

From St Johns Wood to County Hall
Saatchi's been to them all,
Now he wants us to come and see
His new place in Chelsea.

You can still buy Mary Quant
If that's want you want,
But the troops aren't here any more –
Saatchi's shown them the door.

IN THE COUNTRY

The house nestles in the country
Surrounded by fields and a wood.
The sun shines through the windows
Leaving me feeling so very good.

The views go on for miles,
In the distance is a church spire.
During the day my spirits
Get lifted higher and higher.

But at night the house changes
And creatures suddenly appear
From the woods and the fields –
If you listen you can hear

Their strange murmurs and cries
And a tapping on the glass.
Is it a branch blowing in the wind
Or a spirit from my past?

There's a moaning outside
Is it an animal caught in a trap?
The rain pours down in buckets
I hear a thunderclap.

I cannot sleep till dawn
When there is a beautiful sunrise.
The golden rays shine through
As the bird song multiplies

There are bluebells and snowdrops
And the buzz of busy honeybees.
There is a warm gentle breeze
Rustling the green leaves in the trees.

Until night falls again
And the moon is covered by dark clouds,
There is no light at all outside
I swear I can see shrouds,

Are they ghosts, between the trees
Or am I imagining?
The breeze turns into a gale
And sets everything rattling.

They're coming to get me
I'm not sure I can survive,
I'll be very very lucky
If I get out of this place alive.

So the next day I pack my things
I'm heading back to town,
Where I can look out of my window
And see people walking up and down.

Instead of country I'll have my garden,
I'll plant oak, cypress and willow,
And at night there'll be streetlights
So I'll sleep soundly on my
pillow.

THE VENDING MACHINE

I want a bottle of water
There's one in the vending machine,
So I take my place in the queue
More nervous than I've ever been.

People ahead of me choose
And press the button for their Twix,
But I know that when my turn comes
I'll get into an awful fix.

I hope the person in front
Has some sort of vending machine trouble,
But they do it as easy as anything –
I know I'll get into a muddle.

I put my money in the slot
And carefully select the right code,
I wait for a short while
But there's some sort of overload.

Nothing happens, nil, zilch!
My palms are soon full of sweat.
There must be ten people behind me;
I'm sure they're beginning to fret.

They'll start shuffling their feet and sighing
And looking to see what's the delay.
I'm beginning to think I should leave
And come back another day.

But then I decide to try again;
I'll do it the other way round.
I press the refund button; there's a clunk
And my money is there to be found.

In that mysterious little slot
That can make or break your mind.
Will money be refunded or
Will there be nothing to actually find?

God was with me that day –
This time I was lucky
I took the coins, pressed the code
And then I put in the money.

Lo and behold something moved
There were whirrs, clinks and clucks.
Did I get my thirst-quenching water?
No, I got salted peanuts.

CHAPTER 8

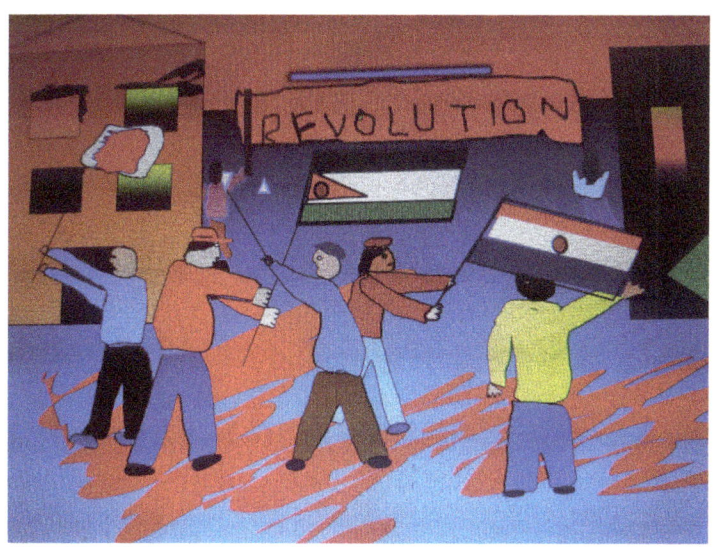

LOCKING THE DOOR AGAINST THE WORLD

I come home and close my front door,
Closing my door against the world.
Away from the danger, away from the harm
Safe in my house, in its enclosing arms.

Away from terrorists, away from bombs,
Away from nasty people.
I shut them out, they can't come in
They can go elsewhere to commit their sin.

But then I get a cold call from someone
Who wants to steal from my account.
The closed door is no aid
Against theft of all that I'm paid.

I come home and close my front door
Closing my door against the world.
Away from the rain, away from the storm
Safe by the fire, so lovely and warm.

Away from the snow, away from the wind,
Away from the frost and ice.
I shut them out and sit by the fire.
What else could I possibly desire?

But then I switch on the TV
To see the evening news,
Seeing stories of woe and misery –
My feeling of well-being is history.

I come home and close my front door
Closing my door against the world.
Away from people who think they're superior
Trying to make me feel inferior.

Away from the remarks, away from the looks,
Away from the people I hate.
I'm alone in my house, there's nobody there
I can sit and dream in my comfortable chair.

But then I turn on the computer
And look at some Facebook pages.
They seem to be having a better time than me
So back comes my feeling of misery.

But then you call and say
Do you want to come out tonight?
So I shut my door and go *into* the world
And suddenly everything is alright.

THE RED BUTTON

Don't ever press the red button-
You'll be sorry if you do.
If you press that red button
There'll be consequences for you.

Don't ever click that red icon-
It has a special effect.
It causes the software to crash
And it's impossible to correct.

Don't ever swipe that red photo-
Because the next one's not very nice.
If you swipe that red photo
It'll come at quite a price.

Don't pull that red lever
On the side of that machine.
If you pull that red lever
Things won't be very clean.

Don't turn that red switch
Underneath the sign that says "Danger".
Unless you want to explain
Yourself to angry stranger.

Don't push that red knob
Underneath the warning sign,
Because you'll find a hand on your shoulder
And it definitely won't be mine.

THE BRIDGE

I saw him on the bridge
On a clear starry night.
Only Father Thames and I
Saw he had given up the fight.

He climbed over the parapet
And looked down at the flowing river.
In anticipating his fate
He gave an involuntary shiver.

But then he saw me
Out of the corner of his eye.
I didn't try to grab him;
I just asked him why

He was doing such a thing?
What had brought him down so far?
I said, come let's discuss it
In the nearest pub or bar.

It seemed a little bit pathetic
To be saying such a thing.
But I couldn't be too sudden
In case it resulted in a fling

Into the murky depths
Of the river flowing so fast
With no chance for a change of mind
That action would be his last.

He said to me, what was the point
Of his life anymore?
His family had rejected him
His job was no more.

What difference would it make
To the world if he wasn't there?
The world would go on turning
And nobody would shed a tear.

I told him that if he did this thing
Here or at any other place,
Tomorrow's sunrise would be less glorious
Without reflecting off his face.

If he could only wait
For the birdsong in the new dawn's light,
His feathered friends would send him a message
Telling him "it will work out alright!"

So I left him just there
Hoping he wouldn't try it again.
That he'd find some other way
To deal with his inner pain.

Many years had gone by
When I saw an article in the news
By the man I'd saved that day –
His life, with joy, had been infused.

He wanted to contact me
To show me how his life had picked up so far.
We had a drink together again
But not in that same fateful bar.

I told him that life is life,
It's not always filled with joy,
But that does not mean that people
Should adopt his original ploy.

Life is to be lived
Until God decides that it's time
To take us to another place, which
Can't be described in a rhyme.

SKYROCKETS

Some people are like skyrockets –
They soar to very great heights.
They light everything up with bright colours
As they head straight up to the moon.

Everyone looks in awe
At the wondrous things they achieve,
But their life is short-lived
And over far too soon.

Some people are like Katherine wheels
Going round making much noise.
You can't fail to notice them
As their sparks fill the air.

They make flashes and bangs
But they're rooted in one place,
And at the end of the day
They've actually got nowhere.

I prefer people like Chinese lanterns
Sedately rising into the sky.
Their flames flicker, are unsure
But they make progress very gently.

You don't know where they're going
Sometimes their light seems to go out.
But they persist, tiny flames
Going on, doggedly, intently.

But eventually they all end up the same –
The flames and sparks will die out.
Before which some have spread their light discreetly
Whilst others went with a bang and a shout.

MY ORNAMENTS

I've got two giraffes and a yacht made of glass
With coloured sails, a coloured hull and a spritely little mast.
I've got elephants in wood and some made out of porcelain
Coming from places to which I'd never go again.

I've got a metal fish from Salzburg and a glass duck from Lake Garda,
I've got a heron made from bronze, a hell of a lot harder.
There's a wooden rabbit from Morocco with its left ear missing
And a Valentine teddy who I think was made for kissing.

I've got two vintage cars from a place you wouldn't believe.
They're from Luton – when I'm home from there I'm relieved.
I've got a coloured dish from Venice and one from Hyde Park,
From Winter Wonderland, so pretty after dark.

I've got a lamplighter by Lladro, which is by far my best piece.
I've got a clock from Bournemouth that sits on my mantelpiece.
There are wooden cats from Canterbury that are on my windowsill.
Watching out for any dog that may come up the slight hill.

I've got a brightly coloured parrot whence I forget it came.
I supposed I'd call it Polly if I had to give it a name.
I've got a vase from Rye of brightly coloured glass.
It deserves a second look whenever you walk past.

I've got glass eggs from Prague and Budapest
Which if pronounced correctly rhymes with "meshed".
I've got a black metal bicycle that I bought in Muswell Hill
When I was going shopping and had some time to kill.

These are my ornaments with stories to tell.
The places they came from I remember very well.
When I switch out the lights and go up the stair
I bet they have a party when I'm not there.

CHAPTER 9

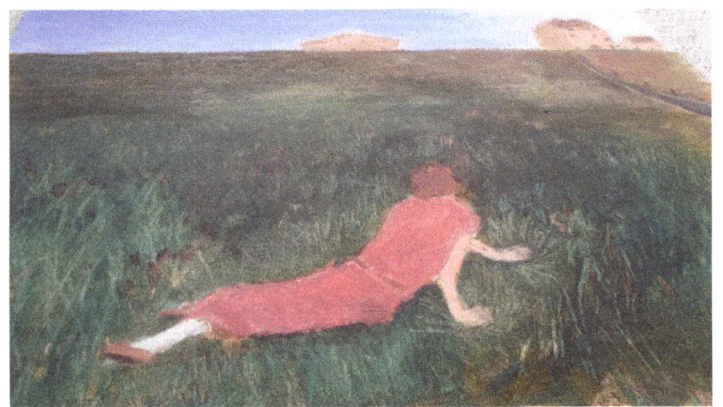

CHRISTINA'S WORLD

She gazes through the long grass
At the home she cannot reach,
Where she was born, where she was bred
It held her present, her future, her past.

They knew she could not walk,
They knew that she was stranded.
Why did they leave her here?
If only she could hear them talk.

She might understand the reason why
She had been abandoned, just left
Trying her best to move
But with tears of frustration to cry.

Christina, oh Christina, who did
This thing to you?
You have been this way all your life
Ever since you were a kid.

Who took away your powers
To walk and move so free,
To go down to the river
And smell the beautiful flowers?

There's nothing to do but lie curled
In the long grass with the crickets
And to watch sunset over the house
That was Christina's world.

MOBILE OBSESSION

You don't ever need to see
The wondrous things all about you –
When they're all there on your smartphone
Within just four inches by two.

You don't need to listen
To what you could hear all around –
You're plugged into your earphones
Hearing some synthetic sound.

You don't need to feel
The atmosphere in a place,
When you've got a phone buzzing
At a very hectic pace.

Why look at that famous person
Who you've only just met;
You'd better check the screen
To see the photo it gets.

Your phone's got all the apps –
You can do whatever you want.
If it's in too small a way,
Just increase the font.

Don't bother about going
To the surgery to see your GP.
Your phone will monitor your health,
And present the prognosis to see.

You don't need to consult
Any library of books.
Wikipedia's on your device
If you care to look.

You don't need to meet friends
To chat face to face.
You can text or Skype;
There's no time to waste.

If you're in a public place
And you find that you're alone,
You can pretend to be busy
By staring at your phone.

So if you're walking along
And the ground opens wide
And you're too busy with your mobile –
You're too occupied.

Down and down you'll tumble,
Apple smartphone and all,
Before it's too late,
Who will you call?

BRUSSELS

He's a European man
Who's come up with a plan,
To make everybody the same
No matter whence they came.

He wants us all to use
And to make sure we don't lose
European bank notes,
And to give him all our votes.

He's already got his say
In many a different way,
But obeying those European rules
Makes us a country of fools.

I've walked past those buildings of glass
With their European flag masts.
Inside there's an army of clerks
Working out where you can and can't park.

They're making rules on health
Which are adding to their wealth,
And rules of safety too
About things we should and shouldn't do.

Their boss is a man
With a permanent tan
From holidays in a sunny nation
In a non-European location.

THE PLANETS

I'm going to build a rocket, to fly to Mars
Away from the lorries, the buses and the cars.
Away from the fighting, away from the wars,
There'll be nothing to fight about, no cause.

I'm going to build a spaceship and go to Venus
There'll be many thousands of miles between us.
I've heard it said that up there it's hot
But there's no danger of being mugged or shot.

I'm going to build a craft that will take me to Pluto;
It's true I'll be stranded like Robinson Crusoe.
There'll be no Facebook, Twitter or text
So I don't have to tell everybody what I'm doing next.

I'm going to build a spacecraft to take me to Saturn.
They say its rings make a nice little pattern,
And if you're worried about how I'll cope,
You can always check through your telescope.

I'm going to build a starship and go to the Milky Way;
To get there it'll take more than a day,
But when you're in the countryside and look up at night
You'll know that what I did was right!

THE PLEASURES OF LIFE

Freshly cut grass, that has just been mowed,
Driving the car on an open road.
A new bar of soap, when I wash my face
A pint of beer, while watching the Boat Race.

Sheets on my bed when they've been freshly washed,
Glasses of wine with some peanuts to nosh.
Shutting my house door when I get home from work,
Watching Birds of a Feather with Pauline Quirke.

When I walk on gravel, the sound of the crunch,
Having peanut butter and crisps for my working lunch.
A freshly charged electric toothbrush,
The weekends, when I don't have to rush.

Lights reflecting on a road shiny and wet,
Arriving abroad when I get off the jet.
Fresh air after being in a stuffy room,
A song with a good catchy tune.

Writing on the first page of a paper pad,
Anything, if it's the best that I had.
Blue ink flowing from my fountain pen,
Hearing rhyming slang from *Strictly's* Len.

The weekend sunshine flooding into my kitchen,
An olde-worlde town like some parts of Hitchin.
The dawn chorus after a sleepless night,
The feeling I get when I know I'm right.

You have to remember the pleasures of life
For when you have troubles and when you have strife.
And the challenge is to find a pleasure that's new;
There – that's what you have to do.

CHAPTER 10

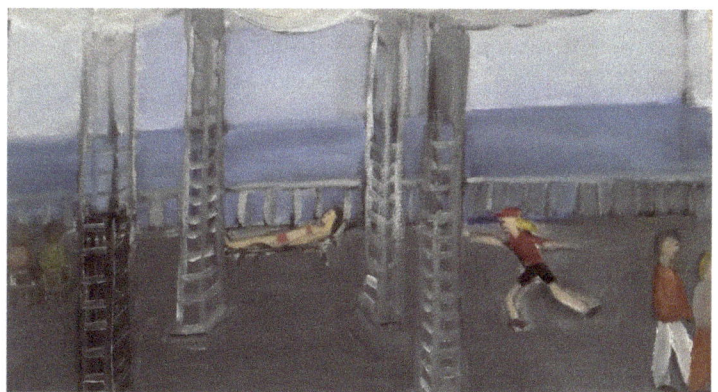

THE PROMENADE DES ANGLAIS

On the Promenade des Anglais
In the middle of the day
The French come out to play,
In many a different way.

Some glide past
On roller skates so fast
Wearing shades of darkened glass
And an attitude of kick-ass.

Some lie flat out, prone
Whilst talking on the phone
Showing plenty of skin and bone
Which you wouldn't want to take home.

Some sit in deckchairs
Normally arranged in pairs,
Discussing their neighbours' affairs
Which are usually with the au pair.

Some people just walk up and down
From the airport to the town,
Past the living statue of the clown
In the hat of red and brown.

On the sunny Cote D'Azur
Where the air is fresh and pure
The girls have a glamorous allure
And of themselves they're very sure.

Some men are in Nice
With girls they call their niece,
With whom they're trying to get a piece
Of action before they decease.

But they don't go near the port
Where there's an undesirable sort
Who have their children taught
That some races are worth nought.

HERE LIES HENRY BLOOMFIELD

Here lies Henry Bloomfield
He died aged fifty-one.
And it rather looks I fear,
That he was missed by no-one.

A tiny plaque lies on the ground
Next to a grand gravestone.
It was so small it could be missed
Lying there, alone.

I brushed away the grass
To read what it had to say,
Maybe it was a pauper's grave
Because there was nobody who could pay.

It just had dates
Of his birth and of his demise,
It had nothing else
Leaving one to sympathise

Because there was no mention at all
Of wife, children or siblings.
No words of honour or praise,
Or any of the normal things.

Money was lavished without care
To enjoy himself while alive
Because when called to his Maker
He wouldn't be bothered with the size

Or colour or material of the stone
Which marked where he lay.
You can't take it with you
Is what he always would say

But the other alternative is
That all his family had died.
There was nobody left to care
No tears which could be cried.

He might have been a person
With no friends to call his own.
He might have spent his days in isolation
And always was alone.

But why was that, we ask?
Was he a horrible person to know?
Did he do terrible things, was he evil
Did he have no kindness to show?

Or did he come from an overseas country
And drop dead in, for him, a foreign land,
Where nobody cared or was bothered
There was no-one to lend a hand?

We'll never know about Henry Bloomfield
Unless we do some research
And ask around the synagogues
Or maybe the local church.

And when we find the truth
About a man probably honourable and good,
We can erect a grand gravestone
Where a tiny plaque once stood.

A WALK THROUGH SARRATT

From Sarratt Bottom to Goldington Hall,
Past cows and sheep and trees so tall;
Through the gently undulating Chiltern Hills,
Like feminine curves if imagine you will.

Past the watercress farm with its flowing channels,
Across the wooden bridge under which the river gurgles;
Past shire horses with fetlocks so thick,
Spotting a pheasant running, whose exit is quick.

Through bluebell woods freshly bloomed,
I took a picture for a couple, then my walk resumed;
Through flooded fields after so much rain,
I do this walk again and again.

Inspecting the Clutterbuck graves in the local graveyard,
Walking across ground sometimes soft, sometimes hard;
Crossing the fields, hoping there's no bull,
Looking at sheep, coats thick with wool.

Driving there in my open-top car,
From my Stanmore home it isn't really far;
Such a pleasant countryside walk,
It's better on my own – no need to talk.

AN AUTUMN STORY

There was a pub in Hampstead
Jack Straw's castle was its name.
Proudly perched on its hilltop site
It had its tradition and its fame.

It had a pretty barmaid
From Australia she did hail.
Her blouse revealed her cleavage
As she pulled my pint of ale.

I journeyed there very often
After a boring working day,
Ostensibly to hear live music;
When it finished I would stay.

Hoping to have a chat
With this beauty behind the bar.
Making conversation
About her homeland, so far.

She was always very busy,
But we did exchange some words.
Then I went away happy
Reliving everything I'd heard.

Then one day in September
When the nights were getting long,
I got off the train at Hampstead,
Shivered, and felt something wrong.

I arrived at Jack Straw's Castle;
She was nowhere to be seen.
I shyly asked a barman about her,
Not wanting to sound too keen.

He told me she had gone –
Back to Australia she did fly.
She'd been sent off by her colleagues,
But to me there'd been no goodbye.

Ah well, I thought
To me she'd been no girlfriend
Although I'd been happy
If that had happened in the end.

So I stepped out of the pub
Into the chilly Hampstead air
Thinking to myself:
My winter's really here.

AUTUMN ARRIVES

Mist in the air
Condensation on the windows.
Leaves turning brown,
Conkers on the ground.

The days shorten,
The nights draw in.
It's dark by nine
Obliterating sunshine.

Long sleeves on shirts,
Trousers instead of shorts.
Got to wear more clothes
To avoid a runny nose.

What happened to summer?
It came round so fast.
Winter's knocking on the door –
Not long now, I'm sure.

The clocks go back,
The evenings get darker.
See the early moon –
It'll be Christmas too soon.

But after Christmas
The days get longer,
But it'll be colder,
And I'll be older.

THOUGHTS

I challenge you to walk past
A person you know in the road
Without thinking about that person
After that brief episode.

Is it just me, or do you think
About them for a while?
About previous dealings you had with them,
And do those feelings make you smile?

Or is your mind filled
With thoughts negative and dark,
About something they said or did
That really left its mark?

And they're doing the same.
You'd better hope you made an impression
That was positive and good
And they're not feeling any aggression.

The world must be filled
With people thinking like this, of others,
As they pass them in some place,
Some enemies, or maybe lovers.

But as somebody once said:
When emotions are very real,
You don't recall what people said or did
But the way they made you feel.

CHAPTER 11

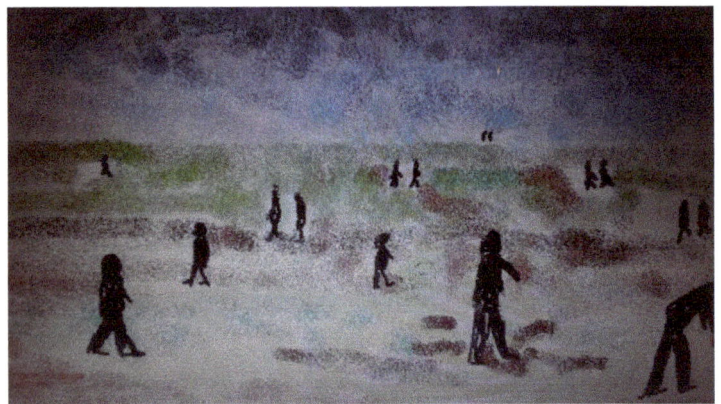

WEEDS IN THE GARDEN OF LIFE

A garden full of beautiful flowers
Will, if unattended, grow to weed.
But if carefully tended, with love,
The flowers will conquer, the bad things will recede.

This world is full of beautiful things;
But the people in it can foment hate,
Bitterness, discord and anger can grow
And if not checked, will overtake.

Like the beautiful building, classical or gothic
Architecturally designed, easy on the eye.
If not maintained will crumble,
Finials tumbling from rooftops high.

Like the beautiful woman, in body and face.
She needs to take care of herself, to exercise,
Or she will lose her appeal,
Her beauty will begin its demise.

Like the beautiful country,
With blue seas lapping at a sandy shore.
If its people are not treated right
There can be a civil war.

So grow the roses, remove the nettles,
Feel the smooth petals, not the sharp thorns.
Grow lilies, orchids, daffodils and tulips,
Such beautiful things will adorn

Our gardens with all their beauty
We can dig out the evil and the strife,
Allowing wondrous things to prosper
To give not death, but fantastic life.

CUTTING DOWN THE TREE

They're cutting me down;
All of me – thirty feet high.
And every cut of the saw
Makes me cry.

I've been here 150 years,
Five times older than these men.
If I spoke I could tell stories
About what happened and when.

They'll put me in that machine,
I'll end up as sawdust.
I hate these people;
There's nobody I can trust.

Except the birds who sheltered
In my leaves so green,
And raised their offspring
Amongst the branches in between.

They're cutting me down
Because of stupid bye-laws.
All to do with restricting light,
As if I was the cause.

They say it interferes
With the children's playground.
Why can't they play on me?
There's fun to be found.

No child can play with sawdust.
That's all that'll be left of me –
A once tall, proud,
Majestic, oak tree.

So when you sit on the stump
That'll be all that will be left of my trunk.
Don't cry for me.
I don't want your spirits sunk.

Just go and plant more trees.
Trees will give pleasure to you.
You can sit in our shade
And lift your spirits, anew.

FLAMING KATY

Oh Flaming Katy, so wonderful atop,
Sometimes orange sometimes pink;
With a crowning glory of different colours,
What is a guy to think?

You thrive during the day
And brighten up my nights.
You're always there for me
As long as you get enough light.

And when I see you spreading,
So sweet and succulent,
I know that it's only for me
That your existence is meant.

As long as I keep you fed
You'll have me in your power.
Sometimes I forget that
Hey, you're just a flower.

ROUTINE

Fish on Monday, meat on Tuesday,
Pizza on Wednesday, like it's always been.
Pasta on Thursday, chicken on Friday;
It's routine.

New moon, crescent moon, full moon –
It's what we've always seen.
The moon circles the earth each month;
It's routine.

Work on Monday, and on Tuesday.
Work until Friday, like a machine.
Rest at the weekend;
It's routine.

Winter, spring, autumn,
Summer intervenes.
We know what clothes to wear;
It's routine.

Childhood, youth, old age
Middle age in between
It's the normal span of life;
It's routine.

Bare branches, then blossom
Eventually leaves, beautifully green,
That's the cycle of nature;

It's routine.
People live, people die
What does it all mean?
If you asked God, would he say:
It's all routine?

BOURNEMOUTH

Out of my back gate, into the Chine,
The stresses go and I feel just fine.
Under the stone bridge, past the kids' playground
Through the tall trees, to the sea I'm bound.

And when I get round the bend
I see the sea at the other end.
It never fails to give me a thrill.
Maybe with you, it also will.

The Chines were once riverbeds
But now they're dry paths instead.
Along which rumbles the little land train
Keeping excited kids entertained.

And when I get to Boscombe pier
The choice I have is very clear.
Left, to the east, is Hengistbury Head,
Or I can go west to Sandbanks instead.

If I decide to the east I'll go,
Past Honeycomb Chine is the way I know.
Along the promenade, past the busy café
Which I think I should visit one day.

Past the surf reef which doesn't work.
Whoever designed it must feel a burk.
Now instead there are exercise machines
Useful if on sport you're keen.

Past Fisherman's walk and the Commodore pub
Where I've drunk pints without any grub.
Refreshing me for the walk past Southbourne
Past a would-be home that I do not mourn.

And when I get to Hengistbury
There is a choice open to me.
I can carry on to Christchurch, by boat
To visit the Priory, with its moat.

Or I can return whence I came
You might think, that's more of the same.
But I can tell you, going the other way
The view is different, more than I can say.

On the way back you see the two piers:
Both Boscombe and Bournemouth piers are there.
If you look carefully you'll see Old Harry's Rocks;
By now Old Harry is sure to be in his box.

So back I go towards my flat,
Sandbanks is further, tomorrow I'll do that.
In the Chine I take the upper level,
By now I'm tired and probably dishevelled.

But not as dishevelled as the down-and-out,
When I pass him I hope he doesn't shout.
There's usually one by my back gate.
I hope it's not for me he waits.

I'm sorry if that takes away the charm,
But I'm sure he doesn't mean me any harm.
That's life, it doesn't matter where
It's what you're always going to hear.

I love Bournemouth, and now it's mine,
At least, my little flat by the Chine.
When the London suburbs get me down
I'll head for Bournemouth, and remove the frown.

THE PLANET OF ODD SOCKS

Here I am on my massive rocket;
This one wouldn't fit into your pocket.
A thousand megatons of thrust,
I just hope there isn't any rust.

I'm on a mission to a distant planet.
Some sceptical people tried to ban it,
But they gave in to pressure from housewives
And bachelors who led busy lives.

You know when you put socks in your washing machine
And you end up with one, where two had been?
Because of that, and other things mislaid
Research was done and a decision made.

It was thought that lost things were teleported,
Even if the laws of physics were thwarted.
Radio telescopes scanned the skies above
To try to find Mrs. Smith's new glove.

A planet was found, in our galaxy
Which was a suitable place for the socks to be.
I volunteered to be the astronaut
So I could retrieve a nice sock I'd bought.

So here I am in my big spaceship
Sitting in a module at the tip,
With a big cargo bay somewhere behind
To bring back the lost things I hope to find.

The journey is long so there's plenty of time
For people to send to this computer of mine
Lists of things that they have lost
However low was their original cost.

Eventually my craft approached its destination
But the radar was showing strange information:
We were descending through a patchy atmosphere,
There was a Next label here and an M&S one there.

We passed through clouds made of underwear
And when the surface got very near
I spotted what looked like black and grey rocks
Which were actually piles of mouldy socks.

These soggy piles ensured my landing was smooth.
I ventured out – not a moment to loose.
I gathered up the socks and loaded my craft;
It was a funny sight, which made me laugh.

But there was plenty more work for me to do.
I consulted the list I received from you.
The list contained things that had been lost
And to this planet had been teleported across.

Behind a rock I found lost keys,
People who lost them incurred fees
Because they were needed to start cars
Without which people couldn't go far.

I ventured a bit further to the crater zone.
In there I saw a thousand lost phones.
Gathering them all up was hard
Especially trying to locate their SIM cards.

Then I searched for the mountain of lost handkerchiefs.
When I got there the sight was beyond belief:
All handkerchiefs were there that had ever been mislaid,
In many colours of every shade.

I loaded up my spacecraft until it was full.
I decided it was time for a gravitational pull
And to take off and head for home
Back to the big cities like London and Rome.

So I programmed my computer, it asked for a passcode.
I couldn't remember it because I've got loads.
When I finally typed it in and read the display
My computer told me we were on our way.

But something was wrong – the destination was Mars;
That's no good, there's no pubs or bars,
And how would I deliver my fantastic load
If I was located in some Martian abode?

Tell them to send me a rescue ship.
The address will be Mars – don't make a slip!
Come and collect me and my pile of lost things.
That pile has so much joy to bring.

CHAPTER 12

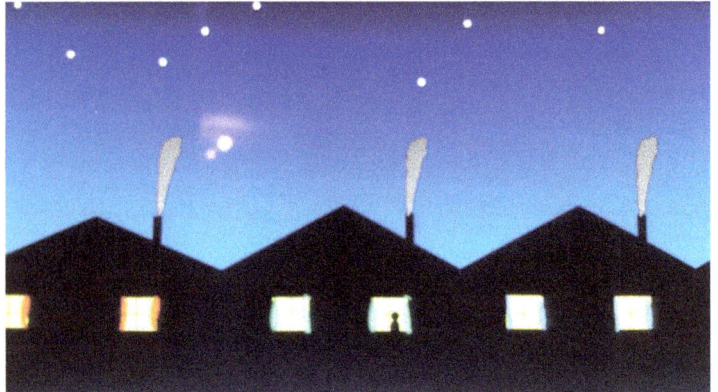

URBAN CREATURES OF THE NIGHT

Screaming in my garden at night,
Panting outside my home.
Something moving down the road, wailing,
Chills me to the bone.

A shoe in the middle of my garden,
Not put there by me,
A gardening glove somewhere else,
From where it's supposed to be.

Who has been walking in my shoe?
Not me, I declare.
Who has been wearing my glove?
How on earth do they dare?

But it's not who, it's what;
Is it animal, spirit or beast?
I'd like to find out, so
Give me a clue at least.

Then I find some evidence,
It sticks to my shoe when I walk.
So it's a living creature of some kind
Who can scream, but not talk.

Urban creatures stalk the night
Doing whatever they do.
But we can sleep on undisturbed;
They've no business with me or you.

THE ORIGINAL MEANING OF TWEET

There's a blackbird sitting in a tree
Wondering what to do next,
When his wife appeared on a branch below
Complaining about the state of their nest.

She thinks the inside could be changed
By adding a different coloured grass.
She tweets her opinion to him
And he knows what to do, at last.

There are two magpies in a tree
Watching the sun go down.
One tweets to the other
"I'm so glad we're not in a town".

Because seeing the sun disappear
Between the branches of tall trees
Is a sight to behold
And never fails to please.

There's a pigeon sitting on a ledge
Of a building in a town,
Perfectly happy that, here
There are no tall trees to be found.

He's a town pigeon with no collar,
Not for him the trees and the field.
He prefers somewhere near humans,
So he can eat what's left of their meal.

An owl was sitting I don't know where
Because it's dark and I couldn't see;
But I heard his lonely hoot
So I knew that he must be

Wondering what to do in the night,
And what that night would bring.
He's sad that it's so dark;
That's why he hoots rather than sings.

COLOURS IN THE NIGHT SKY

Fall, summer leaves!
From those distant trees
So I can see Harrow's green dome
From the back window of my home.

Disperse, rain filled clouds!
I don't want anything to shroud
The cranes with their red lights
So tall, visible by night.

Rise, bright full moon!
And show me very soon
Your luminous disk so white
Chasing away the dark night.

Shine, bright white stars!
And yellow planets, like Mars
And planes blinking red and green
With no hint of where they've been.

Glide past, satellite!
Silent messenger of the night.
Maybe containing a crew
With some secret job to do.

Fall to earth, shooting star!
There's a reason you've come from afar.
I'd like to ask you why
But you burn up in our sky.

The colours of the night
Are a wondrous cheery sight.
You don't need a bright day
To chase the demons away.

MYSTICAL

There's something mystical about tonight
My nerves are all on edge.
There are strange lights in the sky
And murmurings in the hedge.

In my garden, in the gloom
Are shapes I've not seen before.
When it's light they reveal themselves
But in the dark I'm not sure.

A pair of eyes observe me
Luminous points in the dark.
Or are they two different coloured leaves
Or knots in the tree bark.

The wind picks up
Clouds scud across the sky.
The full moon appears for a while
As if it's rather shy.

A leaf bristles across the patio
Wind chimes play a tune.
But there's nobody to hear
Except the stars and moon.

Just me and the Plough,
Just me and Orion's Belt.
Venus is up there too
With a surface hot enough to melt.

Something jumps on the fence –
I wasn't expecting that.
But it isn't anything mystical,
Only next door's cat.

AT PEACE IN NATURE

At peace! Sitting by the lake,
Away from all the stresses, more than I can take.
I'm like any other person, chilling out,
Sitting in the sunshine relaxing, no doubts.

Sitting quietly watching, as insects dart by,
Bees getting nectar, wasps and a fly.
Hurrying, doing their job, no time to hang around.
Past annoying humans sitting without a sound.

It's so peaceful to see the wind in the willows
And the blue sky with clouds that gently billow.
But all that takes energy that makes the air move
And it gives humans an effect which soothes.

Ducks darting, fish leaping,
Insects hovering, branches shaking.
Birds searching everywhere for food
Diving from high to low altitude.

And I'm just sitting staring into space
Think of my place in the human race.
A coot comes up to the edge of the lake
Thinking, "has he got food or is he just a fake?"

Wind blowing, leaves rustling
Animals hiding, birds hustling.
Pond life growing
Water flowing.

I'm just enjoying the sunshine on my face
Not having to keep up a hectic pace
Ignoring the energy that abounds
Making my peaceful world go round.

CHAPTER 13

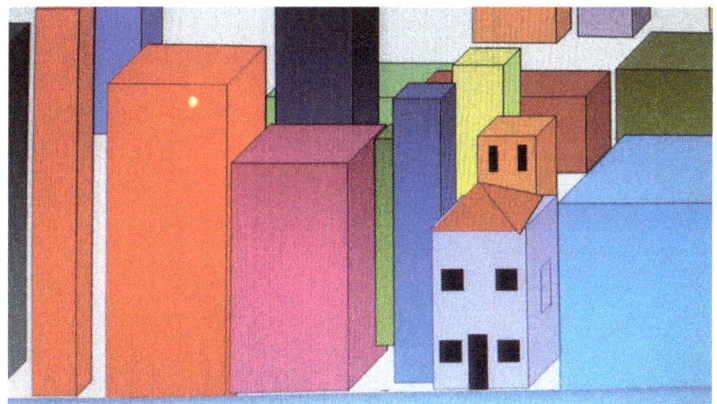

BOXES

If you looked at our planet from space, what would you see?
You wouldn't see people, you have to believe me.
What you would see is boxes, of all shapes and size.
If you're lucky you might see people scurrying inside.

Lots of little boxes, in both hemispheres,
Mainly in cities, there are plenty there.
From the Arctic Circle to lovely villages in Kent
People need their boxes to protect them from the elements

We go into our boxes and come out refreshed
Some of our boxes are better than the rest.
We travel between our boxes, sometimes for miles;
Some are square boxes, some stately piles.

We do things in boxes for the state of the nation
Some people go into boxes seeking explanation.
Sometimes in boxes we make more people
Or pray to gods in boxes with a steeple.

We go into some boxes to be entertained
And come out of the boxes singing a happy refrain
When we leave our boxes we miss them so much
We have to use a smartphone to keep in touch.

For holidays we go from one box to another
Taking risks to get there that make us shudder.
We decorate our boxes with nice things inside,
A source of satisfaction and homely pride.

In some of these boxes our fate is discussed
By high-up people cleverer than us.
And as a result of things they talk about
The people get upset and start to shout.

And then some people get taken away
And put in another box with bars in the way.
So they cannot escape from one box to another –
Maybe the box of their mother or their brother.

I've seen beautiful boxes in faraway lands
Which have been crafted by such talented hands,
Moorish boxes, some baroque or rococo,
Ornamental boxes that put on a show.

In some boxes we're taught words and letters,
In some, people make our health much better.
There are boxes where we go to pray
That the bad things will forever go away.

And at the end of our days there's a box in the ground
Containing our bones, but our soul is not bound –
She floats away but stays quite near
Accompanying those who held us dear.

NATURE WORDS

Flowers, grass, plants so green.
Bushes, trees, air so clean.
Buds, shoots, ponds and sea,
Clouds, sun, so much to see.

Stars, moon, lighting up the night.
Planets, auroras, meteorites.
Constellations light years away
Containing more stars you can say.

Squirrels, magpies, robins and wrens
Foxes, rabbits, so frightened of men.
Hedgehogs, snails, creatures full of slime.
Flies and bees, buzzing all the time.

Daffodils, tulips, colourful roses,
Needing water from garden hoses.
Snowdrops, buttercups, wild bluebells.
Daisies, dandelions, leaves that fell.

Rain, storms, wind and sleet
Cold, ice, giving sliding feet.
Mist, fog, limited visibility,
I'm in front but you can't see me.

Earthquakes, avalanches, tsunami,
Hurricanes, twisters, ripping up trees.
Deserts, marshes, dangerous quagmires,
Heatwaves, burning forest fires.

Nature, so gentle and kind
Why do you sometimes get out of your mind?
God of Nature, so warm and nice,
God of Nature, as cold as ice.

THE MAN AT THE TOP OF THE HILL

I walked up to the top of the hill.
There I met a man.
He stood transfixed looking down at the world.
I asked him what he was waiting for.

This is what he said:
    "I've been waiting all my life for the good things. Good things come to those who wait. So I'm waiting. I'm still waiting. I know they're coming. I stand on this hill and look down at the people – those people who are already enjoying the good things. Scurrying around,

doing their good things. Good things happening all around to them. But not to me. Not yet. Just you wait and see. I know they're coming … I'm waiting … they're coming … I'm waiting …"

"I'm waiting for the spring,
I'm waiting for new life to be born;
Waiting for the blossom on trees,
Waiting for the hay and the corn.

I'm waiting for the seagull's cries,
I'm waiting to see the sea;
Waiting to hear the power of the waves,
Waiting to be set free.

I'm waiting for inspiration,
I'm waiting for my epiphany;
Waiting for the meaning of life
Waiting for its revelation to me.

I'm waiting to find happiness,
I'm waiting to be content;
Waiting for revelations,
Waiting for words heaven-sent.

I'm waiting to acquire wisdom,
I'm waiting to gain total knowledge
Waiting to get to that level of understanding
Waiting for the heavenly college.

I'm waiting to see what the world will do,
I'm waiting for the final war;
Waiting to see if the scriptures were right,
Waiting, because I'm not sure.

I'm waiting to know what I am,
I'm waiting to see the other side;
Waiting for spiritual help,
Waiting for the right guide."

I left him on that hill
Waiting to understand;
I suspected it would not be long
Before all was explained to that man.

CHAPTER 14

Cheryl's Anthology

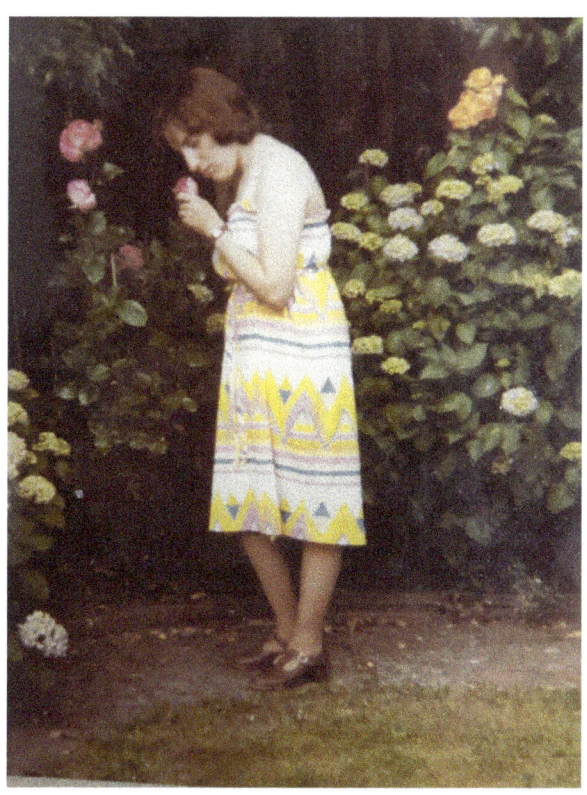

Cheryl Perlow was born in 1960 to my aunt Lillian and Uncle Bernard. My uncle was a respected GP who was a pioneer in the use of acupuncture to help cure illnesses instead of the use of drugs. He had been an army medic during the Second World War, and when he returned to this country after serving overseas, was introduced to my aunt, who came from a family of business people. They tried very hard for a child, but Cheryl was not born until my aunt was in her forties. So she was obviously showered with love and affection by a couple who almost gave up hope of having a child.

It was therefore all the more tragic when Cheryl was knocked down by a car on Regents Park Road in Finchley, north-west London, when she ran across the road to buy some sweets, at the age of eleven. I can remember my mother coming into my bedroom at home to tell me the news. Cheryl was in a coma for many months; when she emerged from the coma it was apparent that she would be severely physically and mentally handicapped for the rest of her life. She would need constant care and attention.

Although she spent the latter years of her life (she died around the age of forty) at homes such as the Jewish Care home in Limes Avenue, Golders Green, it was in the years spent living at home with her parents after the accident which were her most productive poetically. Amazingly, she was able to write only a few years after her accident, from the age of sixteen, although most of her poems were dictated because of the difficulty she had in handwriting. One would have thought that her poems would be bitter diatribes about her bad luck in life; however they were very far from such. Although some poems recognised her disability, they were not gloomy. For example, "Looking in a mirror" recognises the, "small bruised figure of me", but continues in a much more upbeat fashion.

My aunt and uncle were determined to give Cheryl as normal as life as possible. So they took her on many holidays in the UK and abroad, mainly to their beloved Switzerland. Cheryl could not walk unaided, and her parents had to support her as she walked with great difficulty. But they managed to get her onto boats and planes, so that she could enjoy the sights and sounds of foreign climes. It gave her something to think about, as in "Thinking".

Cheryl's parents put in a lot of effort trying to get her poems recognised. They were printed and made into a booklet by the day centre where Cheryl spent some time, called the Flightways Day Centre, which was then in Stag Lane, Kingsbury. My uncle got Cheryl to write letters to Buckingham Palace, Downing Street, stage stars such as Lena Zavaroni, local schools, BBC stars such as the hosts of Blue Peter, Angela Rippon and many others. They all replied, well, not exactly the Queen from Buckingham Palace, but one of her flunkeys. However, she did have more success from Downing Street, in that she did actually meet Margaret Thatcher, although in Finchley rather than Downing Street. I have a photo proudly displayed in my house of Mrs. Thatcher stooping down to shake hands with my cousin. Finchley was, of course, Margaret Thatcher's constituency, and after she died I took my aunt to sign the Book of Condolence at the constituency office in Ballards Lane.

My aunt's stone-setting, a Jewish ceremony held approximately a year after burial, was just a few months ago at the time of writing. As I was saying Kaddish at the grave, as is the Jewish tradition, there was a sense of comfort that all three members of the family were together at last, especially as Cheryl's grave was between the graves of her parents, as if in their comforting arms. Their house in

Finchley has now been sold, and a new family will move in. But I believe a house retains its history. Somehow embedded in those walls there lies recorded firstly the frustrating years of childlessness, then the short period of joy of a child at last playing within the house, and finally the long years of parents doing their best to bring up a broken child, a broken teenager, a broken adult. Physically broken, but not mentally, as the following poems reveal.

HANDICAPPED PEOPLE

It is so terrible to be handicapped –
Be unable to walk,
Some people also
Cannot talk.
They must have courage
To go through each day,
Handicapped people
Must keep cheerful and gay.
If someone handicapped looks sad and depressed
Give them encouragement and they'll do their best.

I AM A BUBBLE

Bubbles, bubbles, floating about
Colourful bubbles being burst
Graceful bubbles floating away
And I am among them,
I've been blown from a babe
Made into a bubble
I'm floating along in the sky
Then suddenly…

From the blue sky I fall,
All of a sudden,
Life seems almost over
And on a rock I burst.

LOOKING IN A MIRROR

Whenever I look into a mirror, I see
The small, bruised figure of me,
But sometimes I pretend,
It's not really me at the other end,
It's a person who can be anything,
Like a queen or a duchess or even a king,
But I like being Cheryl, and Cheryl I'll be,
Because Cheryl I am, and Cheryl is me!

THINKING

I like to think, it's lovely to think
About colours like red, blue and pink.
It's nice to know, wherever you go
You can think all the time
In rain or sunshine.

On holidays by the sea, think about me
Sitting in the sun, think about fun
Like going for a run, or going for a walk
When you talk
And run and play – be happy and gay
Don't be sad – when nothing bad
Has happened to you.

Nothing to do?
Just sit down to tea,
(I love tea time) when you can think
About having a drink.
It's tea time now and
I've got to go,
So Cheerio!!

OH WHAT SHALL I BE WHEN I GROW UP

When I get a bit older
I'll be a bit bolder
I'll choose a job
(So I won't have to rob!!)
I'll have to earn cash
To buy bangers and mash!
But what shall I be?
Shall I be a Teacher?
Or maybe a Preacher?
Shall I be a Nurse?
Ugh! I'm afraid that's worse!
Should I work in a Bank?
No, that's the wrong rank.
Should I work in the Army?
What!! Have I gone barmy?
Shall I become a G.P?
Oh! Don't ask me.
Should I work on the Stage?
No! that's like a cage.
What about a Singer?
But my voice does not linger.

Well, I've years to decide
In which job I would have pride.
But whichever I choose –
I might gain
I might lose.
Now I'm at school
A terrible fool!
For how long will that be?
Till I'm ninety-three!

DECEMBER FROST

The frost is here,
The ground is white,
It looks such a pretty sight.
Oh, it's freezing this year,
Because the December frost is here.
It's too cold to snow,
But still cold gusts of wind blow,
The frost is on the windowpane,
On the roads and in the lane.

I wish the frost would go away,
So I could go outside and play.
The frost is lying in a sheet,
Then suddenly it begins to sleet,
The frost gets covered up.
The freezing cold sleet
Crunches at one's feet.
The bitter coldness seems to go away,
And the snow takes its place for another day.

APRIL WEATHER

The fresh leaves in the trees
Flutter in the breeze.
From behind a cloud
Tremendously proud,
Steps forward the sun –
For she has won
The battle against the rain.
Now she will gain
A chance to make the countryside pretty,
Far away from the city.

Then suddenly out of a cloud
Comes the roar of thunder – loud,
Rain pours down drenching the ground,
Stops after a moment – not a sound!
A beautiful rainbow arches the sky,
With pretty pastel colours to please the eye.
Now look at it whilst it's there –
That delicate rainbow in the air.
For soon it will fade away and go,
The beauty of it will no longer show.
Now the rainbow has gone away,
I hope it will return another day.

CLOUDS

Clouds so white
    in the sky
When it rains
    They seem to cry.

They look so lovely
    floating along
Everything is perfect
    Nothing is wrong
Cotton wool clouds
    On a gorgeous day
Warm sunny days
    In the middle of May
This vast expanse
    Of clouds and sky
What lies beyond it, I ask you why?

FRIENDSHIP

Friendship is important
Everyone should have a friend,
Friends should be sincere
Right up to the end.
Everybody needs a friend
Someone or the other,
If you can't make a friend
At least you've got your mother,
Your mother is a good friend
The best that you have got.
She who brought you up
From when you were a tot?
Someone who's a friend
With a smile on her face,
Someone who has charm
Friendliness and grace.

JOY

Joy is a glorious thing to feel,
It just can't be true, it doesn't seem real.
Whenever you smile, joy comes to you –
It can happen to all – it doesn't matter who!!
Just make it last, if joy comes near,
Be happy and laugh and forget all fear.

About the Author

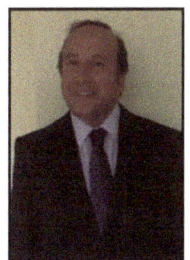

Paul Klinger lives in North West London and has been writing poetry and painting for many years in his spare time.

His profession is in software quality engineering. He has exhibited his paintings locally and has held poetry readings.

www.ingramcontent.com/pod-product-compliance
Lightning Source LLC
Chambersburg PA
CBHW040516220526
45473CB00012B/2885